DATE DUE

MR 2 4 '97			

DEMCO 38-296

Footing the Bill
for Superfund
Cleanups

Footing the Bill for Superfund Cleanups

Who Pays and How?

Katherine N. Probst
Don Fullerton
Robert E. Litan
Paul R. Portney

The Brookings Institution
and
Resources for the Future

Washington, D.C.

© 1995 by
THE BROOKINGS INSTITUTION
1775 Massachusetts Avenue, N.W., Washington, D.C. 20036
and
RESOURCES FOR THE FUTURE
1616 P St., N.W., Washington, D.C. 20036

Library of Congress Cataloging-in-Publication Data

United States. Comprehensive Environmental Response
and Liability Act of 1980.
    Footing the bill for superfund cleanups: who pays and how?
Katherine N. Probst . . . [et al.].
    p.   cm.
Includes bibliographical references and index.
ISBN 0-8157-2994-4. — ISBN 0-8157-2995-2 (pbk.)
    1. Hazardous waste sites—United States—Cleaning—Finance.
I. Probst, Katherine N.
HC110.w3u54   1995
338.4'736337384'0973—dc20   94-37702
                                                                CIP

9 8 7 6 5 4 3 2 1

The paper used in this publication meets the minimum
requirements of the American National Standard for
Information Sciences—Permanence of Paper for Printed
Library Materials, ANSI Z39.48—1984

Set in Garamond #3

Composition by Harlowe Typography, Inc.,
Cottage City, Maryland

Printed by R. R. Donnelley and Sons, Co.,
Harrisonburg, Virginia

THE BROOKINGS INSTITUTION

The Brookings Institution is an independent, nonprofit organization devoted to nonpartisan research, education, and publication in economics, government, foreign policy, and the social sciences generally. Its principal purposes are to aid in the development of sound public policies and to promote public understanding of issues of national importance. The Institution was founded on December 8, 1927, to merge the activities of the Institute for Government Research, founded in 1916, the Institute of Economics, founded in 1922, and the Robert Brookings Graduate School of Economics, founded in 1924.

The Institution maintains a position of neutrality on issues of public policy to safeguard the intellectual freedom of the staff. Interpretations or conclusions in Brookings publications should be understood to be solely those of the authors.

RESOURCES FOR THE FUTURE

Resources for the Future is an independent, nonprofit organization engaged in research and public education on natural resources and environmental issues. Its mission is to create and disseminate knowledge that helps people make better decisions about the conservation and use of their natural resources and the environment. Resources for the Future neither lobbies nor takes positions on current policy issues.

Foreword

FOR THE PAST two years, large manufacturing firms, environmentalists, insurance companies, local citizens' groups, and many others inside and outside government have been debating changes in the Comprehensive Environmental Response, Compensation and Liability Act of 1980 (better known as Superfund), which establishes procedures for identifying and apportioning the costs of cleaning up sites contaminated by hazardous substances. Each group has its favorite reform proposal, and each proposal is put forward with the claim that it will hasten the cleanup of sites, "get the lawyers out of the process," ameliorate a variety of inequities, and cure all manner of statutory ills. Yet few advocates support their claims with careful data and rigorous analysis. This book attempts to remedy that problem.

Focusing on one particularly controversial aspect of Superfund—the liability standards that spell out who can be made to pay for the cleanup of hazardous substances—Katherine Probst, Don Fullerton, Robert Litan, and Paul Portney have analyzed who really bears the economic burdens created under the law. They discuss the initial incidence of the cleanup costs that private parties often have to bear, the transaction costs (legal fees, most prominently) that accompany the cleanup costs, and the special taxes created under the Superfund, as well as the administrative and compliance costs to which the taxes give rise. The authors then show how these burdens are likely to be shifted to other parties. They perform this analysis both for current

Superfund liability standards and taxes and for various proposed changes, including a proposal put forward by the Clinton administration in the 103d Congress.

As the authors state at the outset, this book does not address every aspect of the Superfund law. Nevertheless, it provides a careful and impartial analysis of what is arguably the most divisive issue in the reauthorization debate—who should pay for site cleanups and how.

The research in this book was made possible by generous support from a variety of sources. At Resources for the Future, the research of Katherine Probst and Paul Portney was supported by major grants from the U.S. Environmental Protection Agency through the Office of Policy, Planning and Evaluation (under cooperative agreement CR 815934) and the Office of Solid Waste and Emergency Response (under grant CR 820740). Unrestricted contributions from the many corporations that support the Center for Risk Management at Resources for the Future also helped support this work. At Brookings, Robert Litan and Don Fullerton's research was funded by the Center for Law, Economics and Politics, which received financial support from CSX Corporation; Crum & Forster, Inc.; Honeywell, Inc.; the Reinsurance Association of America; the Starr Foundation; the State Farm Insurance Companies; and the Union Carbide Corporation. Finally, grant funds from the National Science Foundation helped support Don Fullerton's work (under grant SES-9122785) when he was at Carnegie Mellon University.

For constructive comments on early versions of this book, the authors thank Kenneth Abraham, Jan Acton, Amy Bouska, Bill Bresnick, Sue Briggum, Ellen Brown, Toby Clark, Don Clay, Bruce Diamond, Lloyd Dixon, Maryann Froehlich, Lee Fuller, Jerry Hausman, Russell Jones, Martha Judy, Lewis Kornhauser, Alan Krupnick, Marianne Lamont, Elliott Laws, Myrna Lopez, Mort Mullins, Alicia Munnell, Wally Oates, Chris O'Donnell, Ed Pollack, Bruce Pumphrey, Richard Revesz, Earl Salo, Joel Slemrod, Rena Steinzor, John Tilton, and Harriet Tregoning. Tom Barthold, Perry Beider, Dave Evans, Tom Gillis, Peter Merrill, and Mike Miller, provided detailed comments on many drafts.

Kacy Collons, Janet Stone, Karen Terry, Seng-Su Tsang, and Kirsten Wallenstein provided research assistance. Sheryl Huweart, John Mankin, and Anita G. Whitlock typed various sections of the manuscript. Samuel Allen and James R. Schneider edited the manuscript, David Bearce and Laura Kelly verified its factual accuracy, and Julia Petrakis compiled the index.

The views expressed in this book are those of the authors and should not be ascribed to the persons or organizations whose assistance is acknowledged above or to the trustees, officers, or other staff members of Resources for the Future or the Brookings Institution.

Robert W. Fri
President, Resources for the Future

Bruce K. MacLaury
President, Brookings Institution

December 1994
Washington, D.C.

Contents

Tables

Figures

CHAPTER ONE

Introduction and Summary

T HE Comprehensive Environmental Response, Compensation, and Liability Act of 1980 (hereafter referred to as CERCLA or Superfund) is the newest of the seven major environmental statutes under which the Environmental Protection Agency has responsibility for protecting the environment. Arguably, it is the most controversial as well. Complaints about Superfund come from municipal officials, bankers, and the many individuals, corporations, and other entities that have either generated or transported hazardous substances during the past 100 years or that have owned and operated the disposal sites or other facilities where contamination remains. These latter entities—which at some point had some physical connection with the hazardous materials—are likely to be named as *responsible parties* under Superfund, the ones upon whom the initial financial burden of site remediation usually falls. Insurance companies also could find themselves liable for billions of dollars in Superfund cleanup costs, and insurers are already incurring sizable transaction costs. All of these parties have complained loudly about the financial burdens imposed by Superfund.

Dissatisfaction with Superfund is not confined to those liable for cleanup, however. Environmental advocates are displeased with both the slow pace of cleanup under the statute and the impermanence they believe characterizes many cleanups. Many in Congress share these concerns. Even the president of the United States has cast aspersions on the Superfund program, pointing out in both the preinaugural economic summit in Little Rock and again in his first State of the Union message that the Superfund program has to be changed.

With all this dissatisfaction, one might think that reform of Superfund would be straightforward. Not by a long shot. First, although seemingly everyone has a complaint about the program, the provisions that some would like to see relaxed are the same that others believe need to be strengthened, and vice versa. Satisfying one group, then, will only further antagonize another. Second, although some experts believe that the current health and ecological risks at many Superfund sites are negligible or even nonexistent, the public consistently regards such sites as posing a more serious threat than any other environmental problem. Actual data on the nature of these health risks are sketchy at best, according to a report by the National Academy of Sciences.[1]

Third, the Superfund program has become one of the major focal points of concern about environmental justice on the part of minority groups complaining of the perceived inequities of the past two decades of U.S. environmental policy. They maintain that waste disposal facilities have been and continue to be disproportionately sited in minority neighborhoods, and allege also that minorities are given short shrift when decisions are made about which sites to clean up and when. Although we do not address these issues in this book, it is important to note that these concerns have led to heightened sensitivities regarding cleanup and as a consequence will make reform more difficult. A variety of other factors further complicate Superfund reform as well.

One thing everyone will agree on is that the Superfund debate is characterized by much heat but little light. We hope to rectify this situation. The authors of this book include members of two public policy research institutions, each with an interest in the economic ramifications of regulation, and a university-based economist specializing in taxation. The views here are ours and ours alone, of course, but we are not burdened by the need to defend a particular position or ideological point of view. We hope this gives credence to our work.

To be sure, ours is not the only analysis of Superfund; some useful studies already have improved the quality of the debate. For instance, researchers at the RAND Corporation have compiled the first hard data on the legal and other transaction costs incurred to date by several large corporate responsible parties and a handful of insurance companies.[2] A comparable analysis by RAND of the costs to smaller companies was completed in 1993.[3] Another group, this one at the University of Tennessee, conducted the first independent analysis of the costs of cleaning up all hazardous waste sites, including Superfund sites.[4] Recently the Congressional Budget Office, looking over the foreseeable future of the Superfund program, made estimates of the eventual total cost of site remediation for nonfederal sites under a variety of assumptions about numbers of sites, pace of cleanup, and so on.[5] Researchers at the State University of New York at Albany have conducted detailed case studies of a number of site cleanups that shed light on the settlement and enforcement processes.[6] And several of us have contributed to the literature as well, laying out in 1992 the likely pros and cons associated with a variety of possible changes in the liability provisions of Superfund.[7]

To this point, however, no one has taken on what seems to us to be an obvious and important task. Specifically, there has been no analysis of the way in which the sometimes significant economic burdens created under Superfund reverberate throughout the economy. Nor, so far as we can tell, has anyone attempted to analyze carefully the economic effects of the proposed changes to Superfund that are currently under consideration. This is strange in view of the largely economics-based arguments made by many Superfund critics, especially those in the business community.

This book was written to fill that gap. In particular, we try to provide the first comprehensive analysis of the likely eventual economic incidence of the Superfund program. In doing so we concentrate on three economic burdens that arise as a result of Superfund. The first is cleanup costs, the expenses associated with putting in place and implementing a plan to contain or remove the hazardous materials at a site. The second is transaction costs, the legal, consulting, and other expenses that are incurred largely (though not exclusively) as a result of litigation under Superfund. The third burden is taxes, a variety of which were created by Congress to help stock the Superfund trust fund. In each case our goal is to identify who would end up bearing these burdens (hence the title of this book). Moreover, because the major proposals to reform the Superfund program would create new taxes, reallocate cleanup costs from the private sector to the government, and affect (in sometimes conflicting directions) the amount of transaction costs incurred, we analyze carefully several of those proposals as well. We pay particular attention throughout our analysis to several important industries that are especially affected by the Superfund program.

It is worth saying a word about how we have approached our task. We began by assembling what we believe to be one of the most comprehensive databases extant on those sites on the National Priorities List (NPL)—the Environmental Protection Agency's list of contaminated sites most in need of remediation. The 1,320 sites on that list are generally taken to be the worst or most contaminated in the country. For each nonfederal site on the list, we went through six different EPA databases, recording information such as the type of site (municipal landfill or industrial disposal facility, for example), the number of and industrial classification of the responsible parties at the site, and the year that disposal at the site ceased, as well as a number of other bits of information where available. We also built on the research by the University of Tennessee and the RAND Corporation to estimate likely eventual cleanup and transaction costs for each site. Wherever possible, we cross-checked databases against each other. We wish to emphasize here that the analysis in this book does not address the cost of cleaning up facilities owned or operated by federal agencies, notably the Departments of Energy, Defense, and the Interior.

Although our database was developed to allow us to estimate the effects of the alternative liability scenarios discussed in this book, we believe it has great value in and of itself. Debates about Superfund program reform have been conducted in what amounts to a factual vacuum. Proponents of one plan or another talk about the salutary effects their proposal would have on transaction costs, product prices, labor productivity, or competitiveness without ever knowing, as nearly as we can tell, just how many sites would be affected by their proposal. Neither do they indicate how much financial relief their proposal might provide and to whom, nor how these benefits would be spread throughout the economy. Although it is by no means definitive, the database assembled for this book makes it possible for the first time to speak somewhat knowledgeably about a number of these effects.

As a next step, we identified a variety of possible changes in the liability standards that Congress established in the 1980 Superfund statute. These include changes proposed by the Clinton administration in February 1994 and a proposal made about the same time by a coalition of minority groups, insurance companies, and several large corporations. Both proposals would affect the magnitude of cleanup costs as well as the transaction costs borne, at least initially, by responsible parties at Superfund sites. And because our purpose is to examine the economic effects associated not only with changes in Superfund liability but also with the tax increases that would be required to pay for these changes, we analyze a variety of ways to raise the increased revenues required. Among these is the financing system proposed by the Clinton administration as part of its Superfund reform package.

To ascertain the economic consequences of new Superfund taxes or changes in the existing taxes, we needed a model. We elected to use an exceedingly simple approach, making use of the most recent industrial input-output table for the United States. As explained in greater detail in chapter 4, such a table describes (for a particular point in time) how much of the output of industries A through Z in the United States are used to produce the output of each industry, A through Z. Such a table enables us to predict in a crude fashion, for example, the effect on each industry of a change in Superfund tax liability that initially affects the petroleum refining sector. The increased cost of petroleum affects the cost of production in every other industry that uses petroleum, depending on the extent of use. Because petroleum is a major input to chemical production, an increase in costs to petroleum refiners would be felt in the chemical industry. These effects would then be felt in those industries using chemicals as inputs to production, and so on. We use the input-output approach to examine the effects throughout the economy of the proposed tax changes identified in chapter 4.

Understanding Superfund, however, requires that we go beyond this economywide approach. In some cases even small effects on prices resulting from Superfund taxes or cleanup costs could prove harmful. This would be the case, for example, where domestic firms face intense competition from foreign firms not burdened by comparable taxes or site remediation costs. For this reason, then, we single out a handful of industries—including commercial insurance—for which Superfund burdens may be especially significant and discuss them in somewhat greater detail. In doing so, we hope to provide insight into the intense interest these industries have shown in Superfund almost since its inception.

Complicating Factors

To facilitate a reader's clear passage through the following chapters, we identify several subtle issues in advance. For instance, it might seem logical that the model we use to determine how possible changes in Superfund taxes would be passed on through the economy would also be used to determine the eventual incidence of the cleanup and transaction costs associated with the current Superfund law and the possible alternatives to it. We do not, however, and the reason has to do with an important distinction we make in the treatment of business costs. Simply stated, this distinction is that a company held liable for certain cleanup costs will probably not be able to pass those costs on to customers through higher prices because of competition with other companies unencumbered with costs for cleaning up past pollution. In contrast, taxes can more likely be passed on to customers through higher prices because all competitors face the same tax costs.

To illustrate, it is useful to consider some hypothetical company (call it XYZ, Inc.) that incurs cleanup and transaction costs because of its liability at a number of National Priorities List sites. Like most corporations, XYZ also makes annual payments to the government for the corporate environmental income tax (EIT). If XYZ happens to be in either the chemical industry or the petroleum refining industry, it would make additional tax payments each year because of Superfund (see chapter 4). In attempting to determine the eventual incidence of XYZ's Superfund-related expenditures, one might ask, should we not just add its annual Superfund tax payments to some annualized stream of its cleanup and transaction costs and then, using the input-output model, figure out how much of these combined costs would be passed on to the other businesses that purchase XYZ's goods or services? Perhaps surprisingly, the answer is no. We believe that XYZ's cleanup and transaction costs would be borne almost entirely by its shareholders and that the environmental excise taxes that XYZ must pay would be passed on to its customers in the form of higher prices.

To understand this somewhat complicated assessment, one must first recognize the idiosyncratic nature of Superfund liability. It may be true on average that firms in the chemical industry have more exposure to cleanup liability under Superfund than, say, firms in the financial services sector. Nevertheless, within the chemical industry at least some companies have very little cleanup liability at all (especially those that decided years ago to incinerate all their wastes on site rather than ship them elsewhere for disposal). In addition, chemical products are increasingly produced and traded in global markets, and chemical producers in foreign countries have virtually no Superfund-like liability with which to contend. This competition has important implications for passing cleanup costs on to a company's customers.

Suppose that XYZ is a chemical company that did incur substantial cleanup and transaction costs. If it tried to pass on these costs in the form of higher product prices to its customers, other chemical companies (domestic or foreign) unburdened by such liabilities could underprice XYZ and take its business away. And under certain circumstances new companies might even enter the chemical industry because they recognize the opportunity to underprice existing firms trying to recover the costs associated with the cleanup of old sites. Because cleanup liability is not evenly distributed among the companies in any particular industry, and because new entry is often possible, we believe the forces of competition will keep the ultimate burden of cleanup and transaction costs on the shareholders of the affected firms.

By way of contrast, all manufacturers of certain chemicals and all users of petroleum sold in the United States are subject to Superfund taxes. Therefore these costs are likely to be shifted to customers, whether other firms or individuals, in the form of higher costs. In other words, no firm could enter the chemical business and avoid paying the taxes XYZ pays. Thus these tax costs would be reflected in higher prices for intermediate and final products.

What if the industry is not competitive? When neither domestic nor foreign companies can easily enter a product market to compete (for instance, where patent protection gives one firm a virtual monopoly), might it not be possible for the protected firm to pass on at least some of its cleanup and transaction costs in the form of higher prices? We think this is unlikely to happen. If a firm does have some power in a particular product market because of a patent or some other barrier to entry, it should already be exploiting that advantage in its pricing. In other words, it would not need cleanup costs as an excuse to increase prices. Thus whether or not the industry is competitive, we think it unlikely that cleanup costs would be passed forward.

The environmental income tax (actually a corporate income tax set at a very low level) might impose a different burden still. One view in the economics of taxation assumes that this kind of tax is eventually borne by all owners of capital—that is, by anyone with funds to invest. The reason is straightforward. If the government taxes corporate incomes, investors will move their investment funds to other, less highly taxed areas. This would in turn reduce rates of return in these less-taxed areas (since more money would now be available), a process that would continue until the after-tax rates of return in all sectors are equilibrated. Thus, somewhat paradoxically, a tax in one part of the economy may have adverse effects even in areas not directly subject to the tax.

Another view is that the after-tax rate of return to capital is fixed, perhaps because of the availability of funds from international capital markets, at a fixed world interest rate. If this is the case, an extra tax on U.S. owners of capital would prompt them to shift their money overseas until the after-tax rates of return were equalized. For this to happen, before-tax rates of return in the United States would have to increase. The corporate environmental income tax would be reflected in higher costs of production and therefore in output prices. Thus under this view the corporate environmental tax would be passed forward to consumers in the same way as the excise taxes on chemicals and petroleum. We discuss these alternative views more completely in chapter 4.

We go to the trouble of pointing all this out for the following reason. When we analyze the economic impact of Superfund taxes on the chemical and petroleum industries (in chapter 4), we assume these burdens are passed on to consumers in higher prices. Thus we evaluate the various tax schemes in terms of their effects on prices. Earlier, in chapter 3, we discuss the effects of cleanup and transaction costs on responsible parties. We compare these burdens to the profitability of certain industrial sectors rather than to price levels because shareholders of the firms in those industries would bear the brunt of the costs. We hope this explains the asymmetrical treatment of what may seem like almost identical initial economic effects.

Another subtle issue concerns the effects of proposed Superfund reforms on transaction costs. Several of the proposals would limit the liability of responsible parties for cleanup and shift the costs they would have borne to the trust fund instead. On its face, this may seem like a wash: although firms would spend less on cleanup, they would be taxed more heavily to cover the cost of the government cleanup program. There might actually be net savings as a result of such a change, however. As we demonstrate in chapter 3, when Superfund cleanup liability is relaxed, companies would not only spend less money on actual cleanup but might also spend less money litigating. Thus transaction costs could be reduced through Superfund reform, and we attempt to ascertain how great these savings might be for the proposals we consider.

One final point bears mention here. It is not uncommon in discussions of environmental regulation to hear mention of "the" industry position on a particular issue. Virtually everyone understands, however, that the business community is heterogeneous, so glib characterizations suggesting a uniformity of views are often misleading. That is especially true of the debate surrounding Superfund. As our hypothetical example concerning XYZ, Inc., suggests, even within one industry, such as chemicals, some companies have significant cleanup liability and others may have virtually none at all. There are also marked differences among industries with regard to the extent of cleanup liability. Firms in the financial services sector are seldom named as responsible parties at Superfund sites; firms in the wood preserving industry frequently are.

Perhaps the biggest differences in the business community are those separating the insurance industry on the one hand and the manufacturing and other industries that are often responsible parties on the other hand. We explain these differences in some detail in chapter 5, but we raise the issue here so readers will understand the very distinct treatment we give to the insurance and other industries throughout this book.

Summary of Findings

Several principal conclusions emerge from our analysis. First, despite a great deal of rhetoric to the contrary, the cleanup of the 1,134 nonfederal sites currently on EPA's National Priorities List will not impose an overwhelmingly large financial burden on many industries. It is true that for certain industries annual cleanup expenditures as we estimate them would be large in absolute terms. For the chemical industry, for example, annual cleanup costs would be $394 million under the current law. Cleanup-related transaction costs would add another $98 million annually to that, according to our estimates. But relative to annual profits in the industry (in excess of $20 billion recently), these burdens are at least manageable. Burdens seem manageable for most other industries as well, but there are exceptions. For instance, the annual burden of cleanup and liability costs for the mining industry is likely to be quite large in relation to the industry's profitability. Similarly, if property and casualty insurers are held liable for a substantial portion of the cleanup costs of their insureds, and if insurers must book these potential future liabilities against their current reserves, this could have an immediate and significant effect on the price and availability of all insurance.

Second, the three existing Superfund taxes—excise taxes on chemicals and petroleum and a corporate environmental income tax—have an almost imperceptibly small effect on the economy as a whole. Not only do these taxes raise minuscule amounts of money each year in relation to gross domestic product ($1.3 billion in a $6 trillion economy), but they are also broadly distributed throughout the economy so that no one industry is overly burdened. The effect of existing Superfund taxes on product prices is negligible, and this conclusion would not change even if these taxes were increased significantly to stock an enlarged trust fund.

Third, it takes time and money to administer and comply with any tax. For each individual tax, each firm must fill out a full set of forms to calculate a separate tax base. Most of these administrative and compliance costs are fixed, however, and vary little with the tax rate or the amount of revenue raised. In some sense, then, the fewer taxes the better. The Superfund trust fund needs relatively little revenue, yet Superfund legislation has introduced three separate taxes—the chemical feedstocks tax, the petroleum excise tax, and the corporate environmental income tax. The corporate environmental income tax is particularly complicated. It is inefficient in the sense that the annual administrative and compliance costs to which it gives rise may be as large as the revenues it raises. This suggests that a better approach at the inception of the Superfund program in 1980 might have been to use general revenues to create the trust fund. It also suggests that the corporate environmental tax, created in 1986 under the Superfund Amendments and Reauthorization Act, should perhaps have been rethought. Looking ahead, Congress should give thought to these administrative and compliance costs if it considers the addition of still another small tax, such as the tax or taxes that some have proposed as part of an environmental insurance resolution fund (EIRF).

A related point is that reform could make things worse, at least in some ways. It is true that transaction costs associated with the current liability scheme could be reduced by switching to a tax financing approach for Superfund, as proposed under some of the reform options. However, it is possible that even more money would be spent on the costs of collecting the three or four taxes created to stock the trust fund and the EIRF than is spent on transaction costs incurred under the current liability scheme.

Fourth, some proposed changes in the Superfund liability standards would necessitate significant increases (in percentage terms, at least) in Superfund taxes. For instance, total Superfund taxes would more than double—from $1.3 billion to $2.7 billion annually—if liability were lifted for all hazardous substances legally disposed of before 1987 at sites with more than one responsible party (one of the proposals analyzed in this book). By the same token, the changes would significantly reduce the transaction costs to which Superfund liability inevitably gives rise. According to our estimates, these changes would reduce annual transaction costs from about $780 million under the current program to as little as $360 million. If the needed revenues were raised by raising the rate of an existing tax instead of introducing yet another new tax, the additional compliance costs would be small.

Finally, the current Superfund program pales in comparison to other federal environmental regulatory programs in terms of annual economic impact. According to our estimates, annual spending in the United States pursuant to Superfund is about $6 billion, including expenditures by all parts of the federal government and all spending by private parties for cleanup, Superfund taxes, and transaction costs. This $6 billion represents less than 5 percent of the $135 billion spent in the United States each year to comply with all federal environmental regulations. Our point is not that the Superfund program is too small to bother with, or that the program is in fine shape. Neither is the case. But the Superfund debate has been lacking some sense of proportion, we feel, and it is useful to set the record straight.

CHAPTER TWO

The Current Superfund Program

THE ISSUES taken up in this book will be best understood if we first briefly describe the main features and current status of the Superfund program. In subsequent chapters we develop a conceptual framework for examining who is paying for the cleanup of sites on the U.S. Environmental Protection Agency's National Priorities List, and provide some new empirical evidence that addresses these conceptual issues.

A Brief Primer

The Superfund program was created in 1980 when Congress enacted the Comprehensive Environmental Response, Compensation, and Liability Act (CERCLA) to achieve two primary objectives: to identify and clean up sites contaminated with hazardous substances throughout the United States and to assign the costs of cleanup directly to those parties—called responsible parties—who had something to do with the sites. The Superfund program is administered by the U.S. Environmental Protection Agency, which has the authority to compel responsible parties to undertake and pay for site cleanups and to conduct cleanups itself and recover costs afterward.[1] States too play a critical role in implementing the federal Superfund law, although their contributions are not addressed in this book. In addition, most states have their own Superfund laws that govern the cleanup of sites not on the EPA's National Priorities List.[2]

CERCLA created two powerful mechanisms to ensure the cleanup of contaminated sites: liability on the part of a broad category of responsible parties and a hazardous response trust fund. These two elements of Superfund can be referred to as the liability-based and tax-based methods of financing cleanups.

Superfund was amended significantly in 1986 by the Superfund Amendments and Reauthorization Act (SARA). It was also extended without amendment in 1990. The 1986 amendments made major changes in the size of the trust fund and sources of the revenues that replenish it, as well as in the statutory criteria for selecting cleanup remedies at sites. SARA also codified the use of tools, previously developed by EPA, to provide incentives for responsible parties to reach settlement agreements with the government regarding the conduct of cleanups and contributions to the cost of cleanups.

These tools were intended to speed settlements and reduce transaction costs. SARA's provisions allow EPA to release from liability those parties (known as *de minimis* parties) found to be responsible for only a small percentage, by volume and toxicity, of the hazardous substances at a site. SARA's provisions also allow the government to reimburse responsible parties for a portion of cleanup costs at some sites; this is referred to as mixed funding.[3] In addition, SARA established time schedules for EPA to start site studies and cleanup activities, with the goal of accelerating the pace of cleanup.

The 1986 Superfund amendments were originally due to expire in 1991. Sensing that the next reauthorization might be as contentious as that of 1986, Congress extended the current taxing and funding authority in a midnight reauthorization as part of the Omnibus Budget Reconciliation Act of 1990. As things now stand, the authority to spend money under Superfund expired in September 1994 and the taxing authority expires on December 31, 1995. For most environmental statutes, a lapsed authorization makes no real difference in the government's ability to implement the statute. This is not the case with Superfund; if the taxing and funding authorities expire, EPA must take steps to shut down the program as its resources dwindle. This happened when the original law expired at the end of 1985, leading to major program disruption until Congress reauthorized the program in late 1986.

The liability standards embodied in Superfund are almost unprecedented. The courts have held that, under Superfund, liability is retroactive, strict, and often joint and several.[4] Liability is retroactive because it applies to contamination caused by activities that took place before CERCLA was enacted in 1980. Liability is strict because a responsible party is liable even if it was not negligent. When the harm at a site is not divisible, liability is joint and several; that is, the government can hold one or more parties liable for the full costs of cleanup, even if other parties at the site are liable.

The theory is that cleanup should be implemented expeditiously and that wrangling over who is responsible, and for how much, should take place after the site is cleaned up. Responsible parties held jointly and severally liable (those who pay "more than their share") can seek to obtain reimbursement by bringing third-party contribution actions against parties that do not settle with the government. Superfund defines responsible parties who fall under this liability language quite broadly to include generators of hazardous substances at a site, transporters who selected the facility for disposal of hazardous substances, and current and former owners and operators of the site.[5]

In some cases the responsible parties at a site cannot be found, or, if located, are not financially viable. In these situations EPA can and sometimes does use the Superfund trust fund to pick up the costs of the orphan site. The trust fund is also used to finance site studies and cleanups when responsible parties, although identifiable and solvent, have not agreed to pay. A study by the U.S. General Accounting Office reveals that the trust fund also picks up an average of 13 percent of site study and cleanup costs at sites where responsible parties have agreed to do the work.[6] When moneys from the trust fund are used, EPA can then attempt to recover these costs from the site's responsible parties. By the end of the 1993 fiscal year, $728.0 million in costs had been recovered by the government since the program's inception.[7] Such recoveries are likely to continue to provide a relatively small portion of the total trust fund revenues.

During the first five years, total trust fund appropriations were capped at $1.6 billion (or $320 million a year); the appropriations were raised from excise taxes on petroleum and on chemical feedstocks, as well as from general revenues. When Congress reauthorized the program in 1986, the size of the trust fund was quintupled, with annual appropriations now standing at $1.6 billion. Minor changes were also made in the existing taxes, and a new broad-based tax, the corporate environmental income tax, was added to provide additional revenues for the trust fund. In the first thirteen years of the Superfund program, just under $14.3 billion in trust fund revenues was collected from all sources,

Figure 2-1. *Cumulative Trust Fund Revenues, Fiscal Years 1981–93*

Millions of dollars

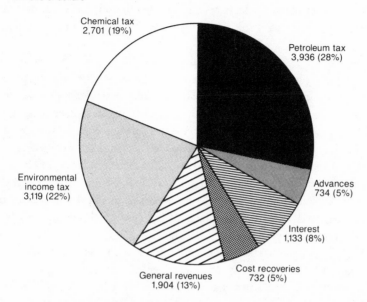

Sources: Data for fiscal years 1981 through 1992 are from statement of Jan Paul Acton, *Oversight of the Superfund Program*, Hearing before the House Committee on Energy and Commerce, Subcommittee on Transportation and Hazardous Materials, 103 Cong. 1 sess. (Government Printing Office, 1993), p. 10. Data for fiscal year 1993 are from U.S. Environmental Protection Agency, "Hazardous Substance Superfund Trust Fund Income Statement for the Period 10/01/92 through 09/30/93" (1993).

and just over $12.1 billion of these funds was appropriated to the Superfund program. Figure 2-1 diagrams the sources of trust fund revenues in the first thirteen years of the program. Almost $10.0 billion was raised through the Superfund taxes, with another $4.3 billion coming from general revenues, cost-recovery actions, and interest on the fund balance.

Under the Superfund statute, EPA has authority to conduct relatively short-term removal actions, which are typically emergency measures designed to eliminate the threat of imminent hazards, as well as longer-term, more permanent cleanups called remedial actions. Most often, the goal of a removal action is to address immediate risks to human health. The goal of the remedial program is more complex and controversial.

The removal program is generally believed to be the unsung success story of the Superfund program. Removal actions, which are limited by law to a cost of $2 million each and to a duration of one year, can be implemented whether or not a site is on the National Priorities List.[8] Typically, a removal action involves fencing off a site to reduce current exposure to the hazard, removing leaking barrels or containers that could easily catch fire and explode, or cleaning up spills or other kinds of surface contamination. As part of a removal action, EPA can provide an alternative source of drinking water if local water supplies have been contaminated.

In contrast, the remedial program aimed at long-term cleanup of contaminated facilities is not considered a success. It is generally agreed that the program was slow to get started and that cleanups take too long.[9] Some believe that the slow pace of cleanup is a direct result of the liability scheme—that is, the need to finance each site on an individual basis. Others argue that major sources of delay in site cleanup are EPA's bureaucratic processes and a lack of clear guidance on cleanup standards. A recent analysis by the Congressional Budget Office suggests that a major factor contributing to delay is the physical complexity of the contaminated sites and the lack of effective technologies to deal with such complexity.[10]

CERCLA spells out the criteria that EPA is to use when selecting site remedies. The agency is to select permanent remedies wherever possible, preferably remedies that involve the treatment rather than the mere containment of hazardous substances. CERCLA also requires the agency to consider a host of state and federal regulations and standards before selecting the standards that each cleanup must achieve. These are known as "applicable or relevant and appropriate requirements," or ARARs.

The application of both state and federal standards was mandated when CERCLA was amended in 1986 and is a major source of controversy. By definition ARARs vary from state to state, leading to inconsistent cleanups across the nation. The application of federal standards not explicitly developed for site cleanups is equally controversial. In some cases, for example, cleanups must reduce contaminants in groundwater to levels required under the Safe Drinking Water Act of 1974 as amended, standards intended to be applied at the tap, not at the point of remediation. Many believe that compliance with ARARs is one of the major factors leading to high cleanup costs, although consistent data regarding the determinants of cleanup costs are not available.

One unique aspect of the Superfund program is that cleanups (both removals and remedial actions) can be implemented either by the responsible parties directly or by the government itself using moneys from the trust fund. In almost all cases where the responsible parties agree to finance site work, the parties responsible conduct the site studies and cleanup activities themselves, with oversight by EPA or state agencies. One incentive for responsible parties to agree to pay for cleanups is that they are able to manage site work. By implementing site studies and cleanups more cost-effectively than the government, they can save millions of dollars. Compared to the federal government, responsible parties are believed to achieve cost savings on the order of 15 to 20 percent when they implement site cleanup.[11] These savings, it is argued, reflect the inherent inefficiencies of large bureaucracies and government contracting requirements.[12]

CERCLA's liability scheme has been extremely effective in minimizing direct government implementation of cleanups and therefore the cost to the trust fund. In most cases in which responsible parties have agreed to take the lead in site studies and cleanup, EPA has not had to resort to litigation. This achievement is credited in large part to retroactive, strict, and joint and several liability. Since 1989, when former EPA administrator William K. Reilly announced that the agency would pursue an "enforcement first" strategy, EPA has increasingly relied on the use of administrative orders under section 106 of CERCLA to compel responsible party actions. Failure to comply with section 106 orders can result in fines of $25,000 a day and possible treble damages. Increasingly, responsible parties are taking the lead in site cleanup activities. In fiscal year 1987, responsible parties took the lead in only 39 percent of remedial actions; by fiscal year 1993, they had taken the lead in 79 percent of these cleanups.[13]

Just as direct cleanup costs are shifted away from the federal government to the responsible parties under Superfund's liability scheme, so too are the transaction costs of allocating cleanup shares among multiple parties. In this regard, Superfund has also been successful. Joint and several liability enables the government to keep its transaction costs low because the subsequent reallocation of costs to other parties, as well as the ensuing transaction costs, take place without government involvement. The net result is that both cleanup and transaction costs fall primarily on the private sector.

A Status Report

Since CERCLA was enacted, the Environmental Protection Agency and the states have investigated almost 38,000 potentially contaminated sites to assess whether cleanup is warranted.[14] More than 3,500 removal actions have been implemented at more than 2,700 sites; 1,320 sites have been placed on the National Priorities List and are considered to be the worst in the country.[15] According to EPA estimates, the eventual cost of cleaning up these sites, excluding the cost of cleaning up the 143 sites on the NPL that are owned and operated by the federal government, would be about $29 billion.[16]

In a 1991 study, researchers at the University of Tennessee estimated the total cost of cleaning up all current and future National Priorities List sites, excluding federal facilities, to be between $105.5 billion and $301.5 billion, assuming there is no change in cleanup policy.[17] An analysis by the Congressional Budget Office in 1994 estimated that the total cost of cleaning up all current and future NPL sites to be from $106.0 billion to $462.9 billion (this has a present worth of $42.2 billion to $120.1 billion).[18]

Pace of Cleanup

Progress in cleaning up National Priorities List sites has been slow. Analysis of recent Environmental Protection Agency data suggests that the average time between the first listing of a site on the NPL and completion of the site's remedy is twelve years.[19] At many sites, groundwater monitoring and other operation and maintenance activities may be required for decades, even after the remedy has been implemented, especially where groundwater is threatened or has been contaminated. It can also take years for the government to recover past costs from responsible parties.

Of the 1,320 sites that were on or had been on the National Priorities List at the end of the 1993 fiscal year, 617 (47 percent) were in the site study or design phase; unless a removal action was implemented, no cleanup activity has been taken at these sites.[20] As of the end of September 1993, only 52 sites (4 percent) had been deleted from the list—that is, EPA determined that no further action was needed at these sites. Remedies had been completed at another 166 sites (13 percent), although many of them may require long-term operation and maintenance, such as pumping contaminated groundwater or periodic monitoring to ensure that contamination does not migrate off-site. At 393 sites (30 percent) cleanup activities were under way. At the end of fiscal year 1993 fully half of all NPL sites had not yet been the subject of long-term cleanup; more than 40 percent had been the subject of removal actions.

These numbers seem small for a program that has been in operation for fourteen years, but the actual accomplishments are even smaller. The U.S. General Accounting Office reported in 1993 that only 60 percent of those sites deemed "construction complete"—that is, where the remedy had been completely implemented—were actually subject to a remedial action. At 19 percent of the sites studied, EPA determined that only a removal action was needed to address an immediate threat; no cleanup action at all was needed at another 21 percent.[21]

Most interested parties, including the Environmental Protection Agency, would agree that the cleanup process takes too long. But there are good reasons for the Superfund program's slow start, among them the fits and starts of the program's early years and the complete halt to the program when CERCLA expired in 1985. By all accounts it was not until 1987 that the Superfund program was again up and running. Also, it has taken time for EPA to collect much-needed information about the kinds of problems found at sites and the methods available for addressing them, as well as to develop a coherent site study and cleanup process. Moreover, as EPA, individual states, and responsible parties gain more experience with the types of contamination typically found at NPL sites and with the technologies available to remedy them, it is becoming clear that to clean up contamination at all sites permanently, as mandated by the law, may not be possible.[22] If cleanups continue at the current pace, cleanup of sites now on the National Priorities List will not be completed until well after the year 2000—and EPA plans to add 75 new sites to the NPL each year. At that rate, the backlog of sites to be cleaned up will only increase.

Cost of Cleanup

The total cost of the Superfund program is another major concern.[23] Little reliable data exist on the costs of site cleanup, for several reasons. One is that most NPL sites are still in the early stages of cleanup, so data are incomplete. Another is that although responsible parties increasingly take the lead in site cleanups, they are not required to report to the government the actual costs they incur, so all estimates of cleanup costs are based on EPA's initial cost estimates and on the actual costs incurred at sites being cleaned up by the fund. But the ultimate cost of cleanup depends on two key factors: the number of sites on the National Priorities List and the average cost of site cleanup. These two factors are only recently beginning to be understood and are still the subject of great uncertainty.

The rate at which new sites have been added to the National Priorities List has fallen off in recent years. In EPA's report to Congress for fiscal year 1990, the agency estimated that 100 new sites would be added annually; current projections call for 75 new sites to be added each year.[24] Most analysts believe that Environmental Protection Agency could not handle a dramatic increase in the number of NPL sites. As a result, most "reasonable" estimates of the eventual size of the NPL tend to fall in the range of 2,000 to 3,000 sites, and most assume that these sites will be cleaned up over the next twenty to thirty years. Differences in the estimated number of sites to be cleaned up under Superfund account for much of the spread among estimates of the total cost of the program. Some believe that the total number of NPL sites is not likely to exceed 3,000 in the next few decades, others say it is likely to be 6,000. On the basis of these estimates, and using an average site cleanup cost of $30 million, the range in total cleanup costs would be enormous—from $90 billion to $180 billion.

The average cost of an NPL site cleanup is also in dispute. The first comprehensive study of site cleanup costs, made by researchers at the University of Tennessee, put the cost at $50 million.[25] More recent analyses of actual site costs by both the Environmental Protection Agency and the Congressional Budget Office put the average cost much lower, around $25 million for each site.[26] We estimate a slightly higher figure of $29.1 million a site to take into account higher site study costs and the present value of operation and maintenance activities that would be incurred for thirty years after site cleanup had been completed.[27] A third factor, the rate at which site cleanups are conducted, does not affect our estimates of total cleanup costs or those of the University of Tennessee study because neither we nor its authors have discounted future cleanup costs.

The pace of cleanups is a critical component, however, of any estimate of annual costs to the economy as well as of any analyses such as the CBO study that discount future costs.[28] The pace of cleanups also has important implications for the level of annual trust fund revenues needed for alternative liability approaches. For example, if total cleanup costs are $30 billion for the current National Priorities List and are spread over ten years, annual expenditures would average $3 billion. If these same costs were incurred over five years, however, annual expenditures would average $6 billion.

As noted earlier, transaction costs, defined as expenditures incurred by responsible parties and their insurers that do not directly contribute to site cleanup, also arise under the Superfund program.[29] Most discussions about transaction costs focus on those costs directly relating to the assignment of financial responsibility: the costs of negotiation and litigation between responsible parties and the government, among responsible parties, and between responsible parties and their insurers. Nonlegal transaction costs, typically the costs incurred when responsible parties conduct their own site studies in parallel with government-funded site investigations, may also be incurred.

If data on the cost of site cleanups are scarce, data on the percentage of costs going to transactional activities are even more so. Two major studies of Superfund-related transaction costs have been conducted by researchers at the RAND Institute for Civil Justice.[30] It is worth reviewing briefly the findings of these two studies and examining their implications for estimating transaction costs for responsible parties at NPL sites.[31]

One RAND study examines the transaction costs, for both NPL and non-NPL sites, of five very large industrial firms with annual revenues of more than $20 billion. RAND researchers found that, on average, transaction costs constituted 19 percent of all outlays to date at the 49 NPL sites at which the five companies were responsible parties.[32] Responsible party transaction costs for the same companies averaged 21 percent over all sites—both NPL and non-NPL sites—with 75 percent of transaction costs going to legal costs.[33]

In a second study of transaction costs, RAND researchers focused on the costs to smaller companies, firms with annual revenues of less than $20 billion, at 18 sites. For companies with annual revenues greater than $100 million, the findings in the second study are similar to those of the first: a 15 percent transaction cost share for those with annual revenues between $100 million and $1 billion, and a 19 percent cost share for those with annual revenues between $1 billion and $20 billion. Transaction cost shares were much higher for still smaller firms: 60 percent of total expenditures for those with annual revenues of less than $100 million. When RAND researchers extrapolated their findings to all responsible party expenditures for their sample of 18 sites, they estimated the average transaction cost share of expenditures up to 1992 to be 32 percent.[34]

It is not surprising that RAND found higher transaction cost shares for smaller companies. Part of the transaction cost share is a fixed cost at each site that is not directly related to the total amount spent on cleanup by each company. Because smaller firms are likely to have spent less in absolute terms than larger ones on site cleanups, a higher percentage of their total costs is likely to be for transaction costs. Larger firms, such as those examined in the earlier RAND study, are more likely to incur substantial cleanup costs. Thus the resulting transaction costs, even if large, constitute a smaller percentage of their total costs. It is important to note that all of RAND's estimates of transaction costs examine the percentage of responsible party transaction costs as compared to total responsible party expenditures. The transaction cost share does not take into account the expenditures of responsible parties in the public sector and trust fund expenditures for site studies and cleanup.

RAND's research examines transaction costs up to the time the reports were written. Most researchers expect the ultimate percentage of costs going to transactional activities to fall over time as sites move into the remedial action phase and more money is spent on cleanup. In a 1993 report, researchers at RAND examined a number of methodologies for estimating the "ultimate transaction cost percentage," that is, the transaction cost share once cleanup is complete. They estimated that the transaction cost share at completion would be somewhere between 19 and 27 percent, "with the most likely estimate currently at the upper end of this range."[35]

We assume that transaction cost shares are more likely to be at the low end of this range because the sites in both RAND studies overrepresent the percentage of multiparty sites—those sites likely to have the largest number of responsible parties and the highest transaction costs—on the National Priorities List. Thus we use assume that responsible party transaction costs average 21 percent of all responsible party expenditures once cleanups are complete.[36]

A third element of Superfund costs is the day-to-day costs to the government of running the Superfund program. These include direct cleanup costs, administrative costs, and transaction costs. Since the program's inception, 46 percent of all trust fund obligations have gone to site study and cleanup activities (figure 2-2). These funds pay for 100 percent of site study and cleanup costs at orphan sites, as well as for a portion of similar costs at most other sites. In fiscal year 1993, 54 percent of trust fund obligations were going to what EPA categorizes as direct response costs, that is, the costs of site studies and cleanup, as well as oversight of responsible parties. Under the CERCLA statute,

Figure 2-2. *Superfund Net Obligations, Fiscal Years 1981–93*

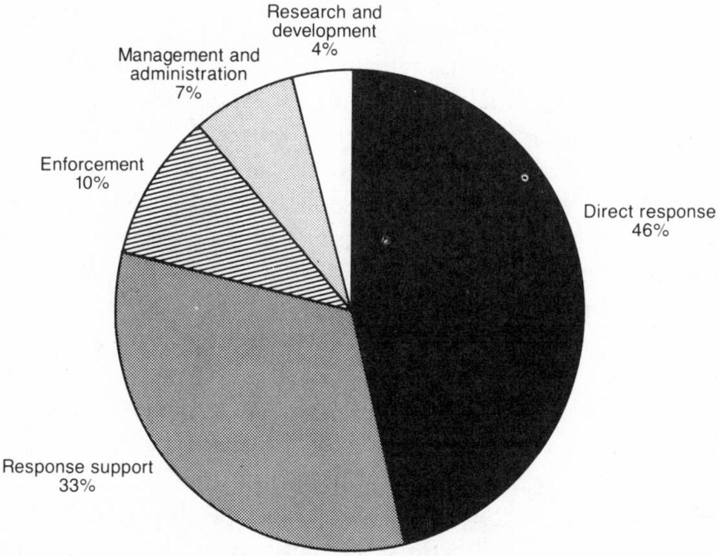

Source: Letter to Katherine Probst from David S. Evans, Office of Solid Waste and Emergency Response, U.S. Environmental Protection Agency, Washington, March 31, 1994, p. 3.

the government may seek to recover many of these costs, as well as indirect costs and the costs of overseeing responsible party activities, from responsible parties at these sites.

In addition to paying for site-specific costs, the trust fund pays for a host of other program-related activities, including the formulation of cleanup standards and guidance, research and development, overall management and administration, and grants to state agencies. The trust fund also picks up the costs of related work conducted by other federal agencies, such as the Department of Justice and the Agency for Toxic Substances and Disease Registry; these management and administrative costs have amounted to 7 percent of trust fund obligations since the program began.

The government itself incurs transaction costs, paid for by the trust fund. These include the cost of the government's enforcement program, that is, the cost of finding responsible parties, negotiating with them, and if necessary bringing legal action to get them to pay for cleanups. EPA's enforcement efforts account for 10 percent of total trust fund obligations to date. Funds for the management and cleanup of federal facilities owned and operated by the Departments of Defense and Energy come from separate appropriations and are not paid for with trust fund moneys.

As long as the trust fund remains at current funding levels, getting responsible parties to take the lead in site studies and remedial actions is critical to achieving cleanups at all NPL sites. To date, the cumulative value of settlements between responsible parties and the government at NPL sites is $8.3 billion.[37] These settlements include payment for expenditures already made at sites as well as the expected costs of future site activities. Few data exist on what kinds of activities are covered under each settlement. In addition, because responsible parties are not required to let EPA know how much they are spending at each site, it is impossible to estimate how much they are actually spending annually on National Priorities List cleanups. Most analysts believe that an upper bound would be the highest annual value of responsible party commitments in recent years—the $1.3 billion in commitments in fiscal year 1992. Adding this to annual trust fund expenditures of $1.6 billion would suggest total Superfund cleanup expenditures (not including private sector transaction costs) of about $3 billion annually for sites currently on the National Priorities List. States, too, contribute part of site cleanup costs. To date, these costs have been insubstantial—approximately $0.1 billion as of the end of fiscal year 1992, according to the Congressional Budget Office.[38]

In sum, despite the age of the Superfund program, we know embarrassingly little about the costs of site cleanup. In part this is because the Environmental Protection Agency has not systematically collected data on costs of cleanup from responsible parties.[39]

With respect to the benefits of cleanup, it is inherently difficult to quantify the reduction in risks to human health that cleanups achieve. This is largely because of the lack of consistent information on the extent of contamination at most Superfund sites, and on the nature of individual exposures. Even if such information did exist, estimating health benefits would be difficult because of the long latency periods of most diseases or other physical harms that could arise from exposure to many hazardous materials. Nor can other benefits of site cleanup, such as ecological and aesthetic gains, be easily quantified. What we do know is that more than 73 million people live within four miles of the sites now on the National Priorities List, that 80 percent of NPL sites are adjacent to residential neighborhoods, and that groundwater is contaminated at more than 85 percent of these sites.[40]

CHAPTER THREE

Liability Alternatives: Who Pays?

T HE QUESTION of just who should pay for Superfund cleanups receives a lot of public attention and is one of the two major issues being debated as Congress considers reauthorization of the Comprehensive Environmental Response, Compensation, and Liability Act (CERCLA) of 1980. Very little is known about who bears the brunt of cleanup costs under the current liability scheme, much less how the distribution of these costs would change under alternative liability approaches. Yet such knowledge is of critical importance to any evaluation of the economic impact of Superfund liability, as well as to discussions of the kind of tax mechanism that should be used to raise additional trust fund revenues should the liability scheme be revised. Each of the liability alternatives being considered would release a different set of responsible parties from liability. Thus some industries might well benefit more from one alternative than from another.

Ascertaining who pays under the current Superfund program is not an easy task, for reasons noted earlier. There is little publicly available information on how much is being spent to clean up the National Priorities List (NPL) sites, much less on who is footing the bill. Terms of settlement agreements are often confidential, making it impossible to estimate the distribution of costs among multiple parties at an individual site. And costs may be reallocated after site studies and cleanups have been completed.

Such cost reallocation can happen in two ways: the government may pay for site studies or cleanup and then seek to recover its costs from responsible parties; or one or several responsible parties may pay for cleanup and seek reimbursement from nonsettling responsible parties or from their insurers. To the extent that insurers are found to be liable under their general liability policies, they are likely to obtain reimbursement from reinsurers. If it is not possible to ascertain precisely how cleanup costs will ultimately be distributed, it is possible to develop estimates of the likely initial distribution of cleanup costs among different sectors of the economy—estimates based on the type of site and the cause of contamination.

This chapter examines two major proposals for changing Superfund's liability scheme discussed in the 1994 congressional debate, and then discusses the key elements of five liability options, including those of the two proposals and of the current Superfund program. The key assumptions and methodology used to estimate the financial implications of the five liability alternatives are then outlined. The resulting estimates of the incidence of cleanup and transaction costs across key sectors of the economy under each of the five liability schemes are presented, as are estimates of how each liability alternative would affect the need for trust fund dollars to pay for site cleanups, assuming no change in the type of cleanup implemented.[1]

A Range of Options

Ever since Superfund was enacted there have been complaints that its liability scheme is unfair and should be changed. Some critics contend that retroactive, strict, and joint and several liability creates large (and wasteful) transaction costs and slows cleanup. Yet others credit Superfund with raising corporate consciousness about the harm caused by improper handling of hazardous substances and by sloppy waste disposal practices, and, more specifically, with providing an effective incentive to minimize the generation of hazardous wastes.[2] Many also point out that the law's far-reaching liability standards provide primary motivation for industry and the public sector alike to clean up contaminated sites not on the National Priorities List.[3] Critics on each side can and do marshal persuasive arguments for changing or preserving the law's liability scheme.

The dilemma facing Congress in 1980 was how to ensure cleanup of contaminated sites (which environmentalists and the public wanted) without creating a new drain on general revenues or raising taxes too much.[4] The answer in 1980 was to make those parties connected with each site—the responsible parties—liable for cleanups. As the courts later held, responsible parties are subject to retroactive, strict, and joint and several liability.

This same dilemma faces Congress today. Many of those subject to Superfund liability want aspects of the law changed, but there is little consensus regarding just what those changes should be. Some groups propose radical changes that would eliminate retroactive liability altogether; others propose keeping the current liability scheme intact but moving toward a program in which liability is allocated on a proportional basis. There are predictable differences in position among key interest groups—large companies, small businesses, insurers, municipal governments, and environmental and community groups—and serious divisions arise within each of these constituencies. Some members of the environmental justice movement, for example, support radical changes in the liability scheme, while other representatives of the environmental community argue passionately for maintaining the current approach.

Congressional Debate on Two Proposals, 1994

In 1989 the American International Group, the largest writer of general liability insurance in the United States, was one of the few companies that publicly sought a change in Superfund's liability standards. Property-casualty insurance companies, although not directly liable under Superfund, face potentially huge liabilities should the courts find that they must pay for cleanup costs incurred by those they insured before the so-called absolute pollution exclusion clause—which clearly exempted insurers from Superfund liability—became standard in commercial general liability policies in 1986. For this reason insurance companies have been at the forefront of those proposing to eliminate retroactive liability. The queue of those seeking liability relief is growing, however.

Two major proposals dominated the 1994 liability reform debate in Congress: a Superfund reform bill proposed by the Clinton administration in February 1994 (H.R. 3800) and an eight-point plan championed by the National Association for the Advancement of Colored People, a plan also supported by an unusual coalition called the Alliance for a Superfund Action Partnership (ASAP) that includes a number of major insurance companies, industrial corporations, small businesses, and local governments.[5]

The Clinton administration's proposal calls for relatively modest changes in the liability scheme and the creation of a new environmental insurance resolution fund (EIRF), to be financed by fees levied on insurance companies.[6] The proposed bill includes provisions to exempt from liability truly small contributors to a site (*de micromis* parties) and to expedite settlements with small contributors of hazardous substances at sites (*de minimis* parties). The administration bill would also limit the liability of responsible parties that generate or transport municipal solid waste.[7]

Perhaps the most major change proposed in H.R. 3800 is a softening of joint and several liability. The administration bill would result in a move toward a de facto proportional liability scheme in many cases. To accomplish this end, a neutral third party would be responsible for allocating liability among responsible parties according to a set of specific factors. The Superfund trust fund would cover the cleanup costs that would otherwise be attributed to those responsible parties who are insolvent or cannot be found—the orphan shares.

The environmental insurance resolution fund, a brainchild of negotiations among a small group of major industrial and insurance companies, is intended to "solve" the insurance problem. There is ample evidence that a large percentage of the transaction costs generated as a result of Superfund relate to disputes between insurers and those they insure over who should pay for cleanups.[8] The EIRF would provide a mechanism for resolving these disputes without litigation. Under the administration proposal, the fund would offer responsible parties who hold insurance policies resolution of CERCLA-related claims in connection with contamination caused by disposal of hazardous substances that took place on or before December 31, 1985. The EIRF would reimburse eligible responsible parties for 20, 40, or 60 percent of their costs, depending on the state in which the claim is brought.[9] Variation in reimbursement by state takes into account differences in state laws and court cases regarding insurer liability for Superfund cleanups.

The eight-point plan called for by the Alliance for a Superfund Action Partnership would eliminate retroactive liability for wastes disposed at multiparty sites before a certain date (which is not specified but would be some time between the enactment of CERCLA on December 11, 1980, and the present) except where that disposal violated laws in effect at the time. The plan calls for new taxes to create a larger trust fund of $3.0 billion to $4.6 billion annually. The taxes would come from doubling the corporate environmental tax and new taxes on insurers and small businesses.

To be sure, other proposals for changing Superfund's liability scheme are being debated. Most are variations on the two proposals just discussed. For example, the Chemical Manufacturers Association proposes switching to a proportional liability system under which responsible parties would be liable only for their share of site contamination; the trust fund would pick up the remaining orphan shares.[10] Other proposals focus on the problems of liability for municipal solid waste and of municipal government liability. The administration proposal would limit the liability of those parties that generate or transport municipal solid waste to an NPL site to 10 percent of site remediation costs. Other proposals call for eliminating liability for all responsible parties at landfills where municipal solid waste and industrial waste are co-disposed.[11] Another proposal seeks to release municipal governments from liability for landfills they own and operate, on the grounds that such landfills offer a public service that municipal governments must provide.[12]

Five Liability Options

There are five liability options evaluated in this book. First is the current Superfund program (status quo, option 1). Second is liability release for all closed co-disposal sites (co-disposal, option 2). Two options that mimic the Alliance for a Superfund Action Partnership are liability release for pre-1980 wastes at multiparty sites (ASAP-1, option 3), and liability release for pre-1987 wastes at multiparty sites (ASAP-2, option 4). Finally, there is the Clinton administration bill (H.R. 3800, option 5). These alternatives reflect many but not all of the major proposals considered as part of the 1994 reauthorization debate.

Many variations on these five options are possible, and many other possible liability approaches could be considered. For example, cutoff dates other than 1980 and 1987 could be selected, or single-party sites could be included in a release from retroactive liability. One could combine options that release a subset of sites or responsible parties from liability (options 2, 3, or 4) with the provision that the trust fund pick up the cost of orphan shares (a component of option 5) at sites where liability is retained.

The options evaluated here are not fleshed out as bona fide legislative proposals with specific statutory language. Many details have been purposely left vague. However, some specific omissions that affect the estimated cost of each alternative are worth mentioning. Not included here are estimates of the likely total cost of damage to natural resources at NPL sites for any option, even though some fear that natural resource damage claims alone could cost billions of dollars. Such estimates are omitted because the claims are still in their infancy and there is no way to develop even crude estimates of the associated costs. Both the administration and ASAP proposals include payment of natural resource damage claims, which would be borne by the EIRF and the trust fund, respectively. Natural resource damages might be costly under the current liability scheme, but in that case the costs could be borne by responsible parties (and by the federal government for federal facilities).

Other costs covered in some legislative proposals but not addressed in the estimates here include compensation of responsible parties and insurers for past cleanup costs and for legal defense costs. Such costs are not included in our estimates of site cleanup costs for key industries because there is no way to assign them to different industry groups. Any of these additional costs would raise the total cost of the various liability alternatives examined here, in some cases substantially. Finally, we do not estimate the magnitude of costs to be paid by state governments, which, as we noted in chapter 2, are relatively small.

Our intention is to suggest the broad outlines of a few liability options and to estimate the likely financial effects of these changes. The relative impact of these costs under each option would likely stay the same, even if additional cost elements were included.

OPTION 1. THE CURRENT SUPERFUND PROGRAM (STATUS QUO). Under the current Superfund law a wide variety of parties may be held liable for the costs of cleaning up sites contaminated by the ongoing or potential release of hazardous substances.[13] As noted before, Superfund liability is retroactive, strict, and often joint and several. Parties who are potentially liable include past and present owners or operators of the sites or both; the individuals, companies, or public agencies that generated the hazardous substances at the sites; those who arranged for the transportation of hazardous substances to the sites; and those who arranged for disposal or treatment of the substances.

Congress gave the Environmental Protection Agency two tools for getting sites cleaned up. The first is the agency's powerful enforcement authority to issue orders or bring legal action (which also has the effect of bringing responsible parties to the table to negotiate with the agency). The second is the trust fund that EPA itself may use to finance cleanups (either at orphan sites where no responsible parties can be found or at other sites) in order to initiate prompt cleanups for which costs would eventually be recouped from responsible parties.[14] In 1992 and 1993, annual trust fund expenditures were approximately $1.6 billion; they fell to $1.5 billion in fiscal year 1994.[15]

OPTION 2. LIABILITY RELEASE FOR ALL CLOSED CO-DISPOSAL SITES (CO-DISPOSAL). Landfills that receive both municipal and industrial solid wastes are referred to as co-disposal facilities.[16] The generators of the wastes at these sites can be local governments or private companies. These are among the sites on the National Priorities List where cost allocation is most contentious. From a practical standpoint, difficulties arise both because of the sheer volume of wastes at many of these sites and because of the problem of linking specific responsible parties with specific wastes. Even where the volume of hazardous substances contributed by private firms and by municipalities is small in relation to the total volume of wastes at a site, cleanups can be extraordinarily expensive because of the large size of some landfills.

Many but not all of these sites also present legal difficulties because they can involve thousands of responsible parties, such as the 4,000 parties identified at the Operating Industries, Inc., site in Los Angeles. Such a large number of responsible parties is the exception rather than rule, however; of the 226 co-disposal sites on the National Priorities List, only 19 percent involve more than 100 responsible parties.[17] In cases in which EPA does not name all the responsible parties at the site, the "unnamed" parties may be named in third-party contribution actions, which may lead to litigation among responsible parties. Co-disposal sites are those at which cost allocation disputes and litigation among responsible parties are most likely.

Under option 2, liability would be waived for all responsible parties, public and private, at landfills that received both industrial and municipal solid wastes and that have ceased operation (that is, closed) before the date on which Superfund is amended.

OPTION 3. LIABILITY RELEASE FOR PRE-1980 WASTES AT MULTI-PARTY SITES (ASAP-1). One of the most common complaints about Superfund is that its retroactive imposition of strict liability is unfair. Responsible parties often point to sites for which they are now liable but at which no hazardous substances have been deposited for many decades and where, they claim, all waste handling and disposal was in compliance with the rules in place at the time. Although the courts have left little doubt about the constitutionality of retroactive liability, its application still rankles many responsible parties.

Under option 3, liability would be waived at multiparty sites on the National Priorities List for all responsible parties who sent wastes to these sites before enactment of CERCLA in December 1980. (For convenience, in this book, a cutoff date of December 31, 1979, has been selected, and wastes deposited before that time are referred to pre-1980 wastes.) This liability waiver would apply to all future NPL sites as well. Responsible parties would continue to retain Superfund liability at all single-party sites and for all wastes disposed of after December 31, 1979 at multiparty sites. Responsible parties would not be released from liability if their waste disposal practices were illegal at the time of disposal.

OPTION 4. LIABILITY RELEASE FOR PRE-1987 WASTES AT MULTI-PARTY SITES (ASAP-2). Some have argued that any elimination of retroactive liability should be keyed to the year 1986. Although Superfund was enacted in 1980, proponents of this cutoff date point out that the framework for regulating hazardous wastes was not fully developed until the Resource Conservation and Recovery Act (RCRA) was amended in 1984 and argue further that Superfund was not in full swing until after its 1986 revision. As a result, responsible parties did not really know what rules they had to comply with until 1986. Critics also contend that before RCRA was fully operational, record keeping at many waste handling and disposal facilities was poor, making cost allocation among parties difficult.[18]

The major proponents of a 1987 cutoff date are insurance companies. It is worth pointing out that 1986 is the same year insurers began writing so-called absolute pollution exclusion language in general liability policies. Thus by absolving responsible parties insured before 1986 from liability at multiparty sites, option 4 would effectively relieve insurers from Superfund liability and related transaction costs at these sites. (For convenience, a cutoff date of December 31, 1986, has been selected; thus this option refers to eliminating liability at pre-1987 multiparty sites.)

Under option 4, liability would be waived at multiparty sites on the National Priorities List for all responsible parties who sent wastes to these sites before December 31, 1986. This liability waiver would apply to all future NPL sites as well. Responsible parties would continue to retain Superfund liability at all single-party sites and, for waste disposed after December 31, 1986, at multiparty sites. Responsible parties would not be released from liability if their waste disposal practices were illegal at the time of disposal.

OPTION 5. THE CLINTON ADMINISTRATION BILL (H.R. 3800). The major provisions of H.R. 3800 are designed to accomplish two goals: reduce private sector transaction costs (for both responsible parties and insurers) and contain liability for small businesses and local governments. In addition, the administration proposal attempts to inject a modicum of fairness into the liability scheme by including specific factors in legislation to guide the allocation of costs among responsible parties. These factors include the toxicity of the hazardous substance deposited and the degree of care exercised by the responsible parties.[19] In order to estimate the costs of this proposal to the trust fund and key sectors of the economy, the provisions of the bill have been somewhat simplified here.

Under option 5 the trust fund would pay for the cost shares of identifiable but insolvent parties (orphan shares) at multiparty sites, estimated by the Environmental Protection Agency to constitute 18 percent of site cleanup costs.[20] There is no way to estimate the financial implications of H.R. 3800's 10 percent cap on liability for generators and transporters of municipal solid waste, or the effect on responsible party commitments of relying on a set of rules to allocate liability among responsible parties, or the extent to which these provisions would overlap with funding the orphan share. Therefore the financial implications of these two provisions are not estimated here; instead, the total trust fund contribution is assumed to be 18 percent, EPA's estimate of the orphan share.

As noted earlier, under H.R. 3800 the proposed environmental insurance resolution fund would pay for 20, 40, or 60 percent of cleanup costs borne by responsible parties for contamination resulting from hazardous substances disposed of before 1986, depending on the state of jurisdiction. In estimating the costs of option 5, we assume that the resolution fund would pay 40 percent (the average reimbursement amount) of cleanup costs.[21] There would be no reimbursement for the costs of remediating contamination from disposal of hazardous substances that took place in 1986 or later.

Estimating the Options' Financial Impacts

What would be the financial consequences for responsible parties of the five approaches? For each liability alternative presented above, we look at three major effects: (1) the distribution of cleanup costs between responsible parties and the trust fund, as well as the effect this distribution has on remaining site cleanup costs; (2) the distribution of cleanup costs among key industry sectors; and (3) the effect on the transaction costs of responsible parties and the incidence of these costs. Our estimates are presented after the methodology used to derive them, and our key assumptions, have been described.

Methodology and Key Assumptions

In an ideal world, site-specific information would be available on the costs of cleanup, the percentage of those costs borne by the trust fund and by specific industry sectors, and actual transaction costs. Perhaps not surprisingly, this information does not exist on a site-by-site basis, in large part because cleanup activities at most sites have not yet been completed and because actual cleanup expenditures by responsible parties are not required to be reported to EPA.

To make possible educated estimates of costs in analyzing the liability alternatives, we used the Resources for the Future National Priorities List Database (RFF NPL Database) described in detail in appendix A. The database includes information on 1,134 nonfederal National Priorities List sites. Much of the data derives from an August 1993 survey conducted by the Environmental Protection Agency to collect information on all NPL sites from staff in EPA's ten regional offices (the Remedial Project Manager survey). The RFF NPL Database augments information from the survey with an earlier database developed by Resources for the Future that itself integrates information from a number of other EPA databases.

We assigned each site in the RFF NPL Database an estimated total cleanup cost, based on the type of facility at the site (such as a chemical manufacturing plant or a landfill) and the likely share of site costs that would be devoted by responsible parties to transaction costs, which would depend on the number of responsible parties at the site. Where possible, financial responsibility at each site is assigned to one or more specific industries (using standard industrial classification codes) on the

Figure 3-1. *National Priorities List Sites, by Site Type*

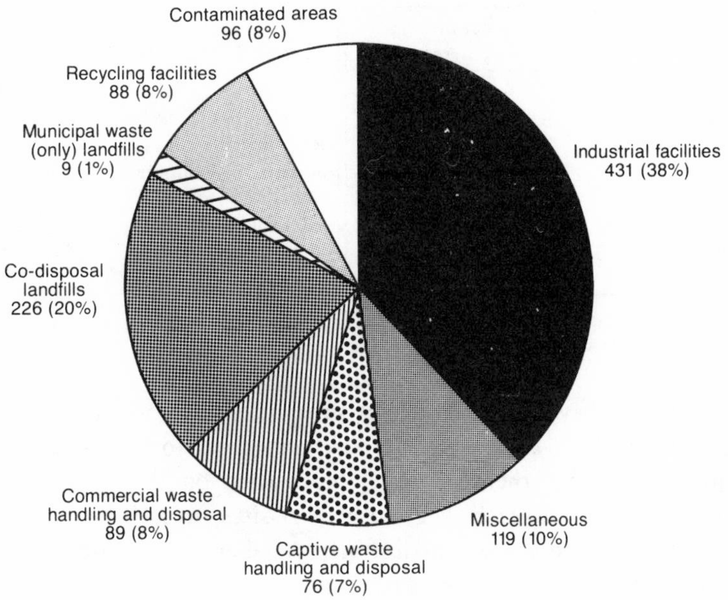

Contaminated areas
96 (8%)

Recycling facilities
88 (8%)

Municipal waste
(only) landfills
9 (1%)

Industrial facilities
431 (38%)

Co-disposal
landfills
226 (20%)

Commercial waste
handling and disposal
89 (8%)

Captive waste
handling and disposal
76 (7%)

Miscellaneous
119 (10%)

Source: RFF NPL Database, 1994.

basis of information about who owns the site and who has contributed hazardous substances to it.

For each NPL site, cleanup costs are assigned to individual industry sectors according to our determination of the industries that are most likely to be held financially liable. For example, we assume that the mining industry would bear the entire cost of cleaning up all mining sites on the National Priorities List and that the chemical industry would bear the cost of cleaning up contamination at sites located at chemical manufacturing facilities. The largest number of NPL sites (38 percent) are industrial facilities (figure 3-1), for which it is relatively easy to assign site costs to a specific industry sector. In the analysis in this chapter the impact of insurance contributions that would defray the costs of responsible parties is not estimated.

For sites at which many firms or government agencies or both have deposited wastes, or for those sites at which no major responsible party can be identified, assigning site costs to specific industries is much more difficult. More than one-third of the NPL sites are landfills, recycling facilities, or waste handling and disposal facilities and thus fall into this category. Most are commercial waste handling and disposal facili-

Table 3-1. *Estimated Average Cleanup Costs, by Type of Site*
Millions of dollars

Site type	Estimated average cost	Site type	Estimated average cost
Asbestos	12.7	Mining	170.4
Chemical manufacturing	41.1	Plating	14.0
Drum recycling	18.9	Radiological tailings	75.4
Electrical	26.4	Surface impoundment	24.9
Landfill	29.0	Waste oil	32.3
Leaking container	34.4	Well field	14.9
Manufacturing	13.5	Wood preserving	40.6
Metalworking	13.0		

Source: Authors' calculations based on E. W. Colglazier, T. Cox, and K. Davis, *Estimating Resource Requirements for NPL Sites* (University of Tennessee, Waste Management Research and Education Institute, December 1991), p. 45. See also appendix A.

ties, that is, they accept hazardous substances from off-site generators. For 230 of these sites we assign cleanup costs to a cross-section of industries because there is some information on the industries that contributed waste to each. For another 147 sites virtually no information is available on the waste contributors; we label costs at such sites "not attributed."[22]

Because it is not possible to make a separate cleanup cost estimate for each site in the data base, estimated average site costs were developed for fifteen different site types (table 3-1).[23] These estimates build on work done by researchers at the University of Tennessee and on studies of cleanup costs conducted by the Environmental Protection Agency and the Congressional Budget Office.[24] We used a government average site cleanup cost of $29.1 million as a basis for our estimates. Our estimates include the cost of site studies ($4.2 million), cleanup actions ($22.0 million), and operations and maintenance activities ($2.9 million).[25] Estimated average cleanup costs vary widely for the different types, from $170.4 million for mining sites to $12.7 million for asbestos sites. Once the industry that is likely to bear the initial cost of a site cleanup was identified, we then summed all site costs assigned to each industry to arrive at a total industry cleanup cost.

A recent analysis of actual cleanups at Department of Energy sites found dramatic cost savings when cleanups were conducted by the private sector instead of the federal government.[26] To take this apparent private sector efficiency into account, we assumed a 20 percent cost savings (or discount) when responsible parties conduct NPL site cleanups.[27] In other words, if all cleanups were implemented by responsible parties, the average cost of an NPL site cleanup would be $23.3 million, approximately $6.0 million (20 percent) less than the government average of $29.1 million.

For each site where responsible parties pay for some or all of site cleanup costs, we estimated responsible party transaction costs. Lacking site-specific data on transaction costs, we assumed they are related to the number of responsible parties at the site and that the percentage of site costs attributable to transaction costs increases with the number of responsible parties.[28] Our estimates of transaction costs range from 5 percent of total responsible party costs (the sum of cleanup and transaction costs) for sites with one responsible party to 30 percent of total costs for sites with more than fifty.

Number of responsible parties	*Transaction cost as percent of total cost*
Orphan	0
1	5
2–10	20
11–50	25
More than 50	30
Unknown	15

Our data indicate that almost 60 percent of nonfederal National Priorities List sites have 10 or fewer responsible parties and that fewer than 15 percent of the sites have more than 100 (figure 3-2).

Because we estimate transaction costs as a percentage of the total costs incurred by responsible parties, the transaction cost share under each liability option decreases in direct relationship to the total costs paid for by responsible parties. That is, the more cleanups that are paid for by the trust fund, the lower the total transaction costs.

We quantify only the likely reductions in private sector transaction costs to responsible parties if each of the liability alternatives were implemented. We do not estimate the cost of possible increases in transaction costs that might be incurred under each of the four alternatives to the status quo. For example, if responsible parties were released from Superfund liability for all hazardous substances disposed of at multiparty sites before a specified date (as they would be under options 3 and 4), there would probably be increased litigation in which some responsible parties would argue that they really had disposed of their hazardous substances before the cutoff date. Similarly, under the ASAP proposal liability would be retained for waste disposal that was in violation of the rules and regulations at the time of disposal. Such a

Figure 3-2. *Estimated Distribution of National Priorities List Sites (1,134 Sites), by Number of Responsible Parties*

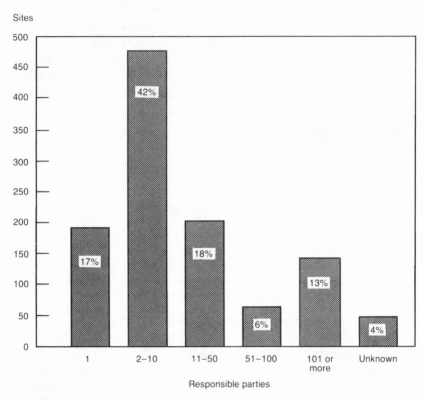

Source: RFF NPL Database, 1994.

legal standard is much higher than that required under the current Superfund law and would likely lead to much higher transaction costs for those sites where there is litigation over what was legal and what was not.

Many of the current legislative proposals that release responsible parties from liability include a provision requiring the government to reimburse them (and insurers) for costs incurred in the past under the current liability standards, usually by a credit against future taxes. This requirement would involve new administrative costs to document what costs have been incurred by responsible parties or insurers. (In addition, providing such a credit would mean that tax rates would have to be higher than in most estimates because some of the revenue estimates would be offset by these credits.)

A number of the legislative alternatives that would decrease private sector transaction costs, such as having the trust fund pay for orphan shares, would impose new responsibilities on the public sector that would increase its administrative costs. We do not estimate these additional costs. Some analysts have suggested that any decrease in private sector transaction costs might be offset by the resulting increase in public sector administrative costs.[29] If this is the case, changing liability schemes will have little or no effect on transaction costs from a societal perspective.

The cost estimates given in this chapter are for future cleanup and transaction costs for 1,134 nonfederal NPL sites. These estimates are confined to the current National Priorities List for two reasons. First, our estimates of the cost and financial impact of the options on key industries are developed on the basis of the site-specific data described earlier. Second, there is no way to know which industries might be involved at future sites or to predict the characteristics of sites that might be added to the NPL.

Because we are looking at current National Priorities List sites, we also take into account money spent to date on site studies and cleanup by the government (trust fund dollars) and by responsible parties. Thus the estimates presented in this chapter are for the remaining costs of cleaning up the 1,134 NPL sites in our database. So far, the government (the trust fund) has spent more on site studies and cleanups at NPL sites than have responsible parties. According to EPA, more than $4.0 billion in trust fund moneys had been spent on site studies and cleanups at NPL sites as of the end of fiscal year 1993.[30] As noted earlier, however, data on what responsible parties have actually spent is not readily available. We have assumed that responsible parties had spent $2.9 billion as of the end of fiscal year 1993 on site studies and cleanup at NPL sites (see appendix B). Thus at the end of fiscal 1993, trust fund expenditures accounted for 58 percent of the moneys spent by both the government and responsible parties on site studies and cleanup activities at National Priorities List sites.[31]

The Financial Impact of Alternative Liability Options

In evaluating the five liability schemes, we look at the distribution of total remaining cleanup costs between responsible parties and the trust fund, the distribution of cleanup costs among key industries, and the impact of each alternative on total transaction costs and the distribution of these costs among industries.[32] The estimates of cleanup costs do not include the day-to-day costs of operating the Superfund program, which amount to about $1 billion annually.

Our analysis focuses primarily on the annual costs associated with each liability alternative rather than on the cumulative costs because we must estimate needed annual trust fund revenues. We arrive at annual costs quite simply—by dividing by ten our estimate of the remaining cleanup and transaction costs for the current National Priorities List sites. By averaging the remaining costs of cleaning up the current NPL over the next ten years, we assume that the minimum site cleanup duration would be ten years (for a site listed in 1994) and that the maximum would be twenty-four (for sites listed in 1980 but not completed until ten years from 1994). This time period does not include future operation and maintenance activities, which would take place after the remedy is fully implemented.

DISTRIBUTION OF CLEANUP COSTS BETWEEN RESPONSIBLE PARTIES AND THE TRUST FUND. Under the current Superfund program (option 1) the remaining cost of cleaning up all nonfederal NPL sites is $21.4 billion (or $18.4 billion in discounted costs, using a 4 percent annual discount rate), or $2.1 billion annually. Twenty-seven percent of cleanup costs would be paid for by the trust fund. These moneys pay for 100 percent of the cleanup cost for 84 orphan sites. The trust fund also covers just under 25 percent of the costs of cleanup at all other sites, because many sites start out with some site studies and cleanup activities paid for by the trust fund.[33] Although responsible parties often take the lead in site cleanups, in most cases they do not pay 100 percent of cleanup costs.[34]

Required trust fund revenues are significantly larger for each of the liability alternatives than for the status quo (figure 3-3). This is to be expected because options 2 through 5 exempt certain kinds of sites or parties at those sites from liability, thus increasing the share of cleanup costs to be shouldered by the trust fund.

Trust fund expenditures for site cleanups increase from 27 percent of cleanup costs under option 1 to 48 percent under option 2. Under option 2 the trust fund pays for the costs of cleaning up 220 co-disposal facilities as well as the cleanup costs paid for under option 1 (status quo).[35] Shifting implementation of cleanup at these 220 sites to the government results in an increase of $1.0 billion in the cleanup bill (because of the assumed relative inefficiency of government cleanups),

Figure 3-3. *Distribution of Remaining Cleanup Costs among Responsible Parties, Trust Fund, and the EIRF under Five Options*

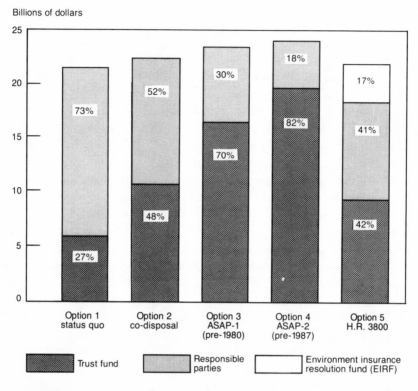

Billions of dollars

| | Option 1 status quo | Option 2 co-disposal | Option 3 ASAP-1 (pre-1980) | Option 4 ASAP-2 (pre-1987) | Option 5 H.R. 3800 |

Trust fund   Responsible parties   Environment insurance resolution fund (EIRF)

Source: RFF NPL Database, 1994.

bringing total remaining cleanup costs under option 2 to $22.4 billion, compared with $21.4 billion for option 1.

The additional costs to the trust fund jump dramatically relative to costs under the status quo if retroactive liability is eliminated at multiparty sites for hazardous substances legally disposed of before 1980 and 1987, as in options 3 and 4, respectively. Under option 3, trust fund revenues pay for 70 percent of total remaining cleanup costs, or $16.4 billion. This increase in government-implemented cleanups results in a $2 billion increase in the total remaining cleanup bill, as compared with option 1 costs. Moving the date for elimination of retroactive liability at multiparty sites to 1987 would mean that an additional $3.4 billion in cleanup costs is paid by the trust fund. Under option 4, responsible parties pay only 18 percent of the cleanup bill, or $4.4 billion. Total remaining cleanup costs increase by almost $3 billion (the largest increase of any option we examine), compared with costs under the status quo because many more cleanups are implemented by the government.

Assessing the distribution of costs under the Clinton administration bill (option 5) is a two-step process. We first estimate the effect of changes in liability on the trust fund, then estimate the effect on responsible parties of reimbursement from the environmental insurance resolution fund. As compared with status quo costs, the trust fund share of cleanup costs increases by $3.5 billion to a total of 42 percent of remaining cleanup costs. This increase is to cover the cost of orphan shares that would otherwise be allocated to identifiable but insolvent parties at multiparty sites.[36] Although this cost represents a large increase in the responsibility borne by the trust fund, it is a much smaller burden on the trust fund than would be required under options 3 and 4. Trust fund responsibility could be even larger under H.R. 3800 if the 10 percent cap on generators and transporters of municipal solid waste results in additional orphan shares.

Under option 5, responsible parties are responsible for 58 percent of remaining cleanup costs, or $12.8 billion. However, 29 percent of these costs ($3.7 billion) would be reimbursed by the environmental insurance resolution fund, leaving responsible parties with 41 percent of total remaining cleanup costs, or $9.1 billion.[37] The EIRF would have to cover 17 percent of cleanup costs, or $3.7 billion, over ten years. On an annual basis the administration bill (option 5) would require $935.5 million in trust fund dollars, not including other program costs (table 3-2). The EIRF would pay for $367.5 million in site study and cleanup costs for the current NPL each year. Annual responsible party expenditures for site cleanup costs would be $911.1 million.

It is worth reiterating that these estimates do not include either payments for natural resource damages (which could amount to billions of dollars) or payments for any sites added to the NPL in the future. Nor do these estimates include the costs of compensating responsible parties or their insurers for past costs or the day-to-day costs of implementing the Superfund program. In other words, these are truly lower-bound estimates of the remaining costs of Superfund cleanups under various options.

DISTRIBUTION OF CLEANUP COSTS AMONG MAJOR INDUSTRY SECTORS. According to our analysis, under option 1 (the status quo), the chemical and allied products industry bears the largest share of total

Table 3-2. *Estimated Annual Cleanup Costs under Five Options*[a]
Millions of dollars unless otherwise specified

Option	Financing mechanism			Total cleanup costs
	Liability	Trust fund	EIRF	
Option 1 status quo	1,559.1 (73)	585.0 (27)	. . .	2,144.1 (100)
Option 2 co-disposal	1,173.1 (52)	1,067.4 (48)	. . .	2,240.5 (100)
Option 3 ASAP-I (pre-1980)	711.8 (30)	1,644.0 (70)	. . .	2,355.8 (100)
Option 4 ASAP-2 (pre-1987)	443.0 (18)	1,980.0 (82)	. . .	2,423.0 (100)
Option 5 H.R. 3800	911.1 (41)	935.5 (42)	367.5 (17)	2,214.1 (100)

Source: RFF NPL Database, 1994.
a. Numbers in parentheses are percentages.

cleanup costs of any industry—25 percent, or $394.4 million of the $1.6 billion in total remaining cleanup costs to be borne annually by responsible parties. This is not surprising because, by our accounting, 8 percent of the nonfederal NPL sites are chemical manufacturing sites, where the estimated average site cleanup cost is slightly above average at $41.1 million. The next largest share, 11 percent of the cleanup cost, or $174.5 million, is borne by the mining industry. Recycling facilities, such as battery and oil recyclers, account for another 10 percent of remaining cleanup costs. After that, costs are distributed fairly evenly among several other key industrial sectors (table 3-3).

Under the four other liability options, the chemical and allied products industry also bears the largest share of any industry, although the percentage for which it is responsible increases slightly under options 3 and 4, to 26 and 27 percent respectively, when compared with costs under the status quo. This comparison is true across the board, as the relative contribution of the trust fund, and of the EIRF in option 5, increases.

Not surprisingly, all industry sectors see a decrease in their annual cleanup costs under all alternative liability schemes when compared with the status quo. For example, the estimated cost borne by the mining industry is highest under option 1, at $174.5 million annually, but falls to $54.8 million annually under option 4, in which we assume that responsible parties are released from liability for hazardous sub-

Table 3-3. *Estimated Annual Responsible Party Cleanup Costs, by Industrial Sector, under Five Options*[a]
Millions of dollars unless otherwise specified

Industry	Option 1 status quo	Option 2 co-disposal	Option 3 ASAP-1 (pre-1980)	Option 4 ASAP-2 (pre-1987)	Option 5 H.R. 3800
Mining[b]	174.5 (11)	160.5 (14)	73.2 (10)	54.8 (12)	103.6 (11)
Lumber and wood products, except furniture[b]	98.1 (6)	91.0 (8)	44.2 (6)	28.8 (7)	57.6 (6)
Chemicals and allied products [b]	394.4 (25)	296.2 (25)	187.7 (26)	119.7 (27)	229.5 (25)
Petroleum refining and related industries[b]	75.3 (5)	44.4 (4)	30.7 (4)	17.1 (4)	43.2 (5)
Primary metals industries[b]	118.0 (8)	104.9 (9)	55.7 (8)	38.2 (9)	71.6 (8)
Fabricated metal products, except machinery and transportation equipment[b]	79.7 (5)	62.7 (5)	42.4 (6)	27.8 (6)	48.3 (5)
Electronic and other electrical equipment and components, except computer equipment[b]	57.7 (4)	48.7 (4)	32.2 (5)	20.5 (5)	34.6 (4)
All other manufacturing[b]	94.7 (6)	68.9 (6)	45.0 (6)	27.9 (6)	55.0 (6)
Miscellaneous[c]	91.4 (6)	64.1 (5)	45.9 (6)	28.6 (6)	54.2 (6)
Recycling[d]	157.9 (10)	141.3 (12)	69.3 (10)	28.4 (6)	87.9 (10)
Not attributed	217.4 (14)	90.5 (8)	85.5 (12)	51.2 (12)	125.5 (14)
Annual responsible party cleanup cost[e]	1,559.1 (100)	1,173.1 (100)	711.8 (100)	443.0 (100)	911.1 (100)

Source: RFF NPL Database, 1994.
a. Numbers in parentheses are percentages.
b. Industry sector based on Office of Management and Budget, *Standard Industrial Classification Manual* (Springfield, Va.: National Technical Information Service, 1987).
b. Includes all standard industrial classification (SIC) codes not specifically broken out, such as transportation, services, and public administration.
d. Category developed by Resources for the Future to classify activities not captured by the SIC; see appendix A.
e. Numbers may not add because of rounding.

stances disposed of legally before 1987 at multiparty sites. Under option 2 the mining industry sees only a slight decrease, $14.0 million, in its annual cleanup costs. The mining industry's financial burden for cleanup is cut by more than half for option 3, under which responsible parties are assumed to be released from liability for hazardous substances disposed of legally before 1980 at multiparty sites. Under option 5 (H.R. 3800) the industry would pay more for cleanup than it would under options 3 or 4, but still would pay considerably less than under the current Superfund law or under option 2.

Each industry category sees some reduction in cleanup costs under option 2, which releases responsible parties from liability at co-disposal sites. The most dramatic reductions, however, occur under options 3 and 4. For example, the cleanup cost borne by the chemical and allied products industry falls from $394.4 million annually under the status quo to $187.7 million under option 3 and to $119.7 million under option 4. These reduced costs must be examined in the context of any increased taxes on the chemical industry that would pay to finance an increased trust fund. Under option 5 the chemical and allied products industry cost is reduced as well, to $229.5 million. This pattern is repeated for all industry sectors.

EFFECT ON TOTAL PRIVATE SECTOR TRANSACTION COSTS AND DISTRIBUTION OF THOSE COSTS AMONG INDUSTRIES. The magnitude of transaction costs incurred by responsible parties can be looked at in two ways. The first approach, used by RAND in its two reports, is to compare transaction costs to total site costs (the sum of site study and cleanup costs and transaction costs) incurred by responsible parties. The share of transaction costs that results is often erroneously applied to estimates of the total cost of cleaning up National Priority List sites, that is, the costs incurred by both the trust fund and responsible parties. This latter approach, which compares responsible party transaction costs to total costs incurred for NPL sites, yields a lower transaction cost share.

Responsible party transaction costs are compared to total costs borne by responsible parties (the RAND approach) under each option in figure 3-4. When viewed in this light, the transaction cost share for responsible parties does not change much from one alternative to another, although the absolute dollar value of both transaction costs and total site costs does vary substantially. The transaction cost share under option 1 is 21 percent, which is consistent with estimates made by researchers at RAND and discussed in chapter 2. Transaction cost shares range

Figure 3-4. *Estimated Annual Responsible Party Cleanup and Transaction Costs under Five Options*

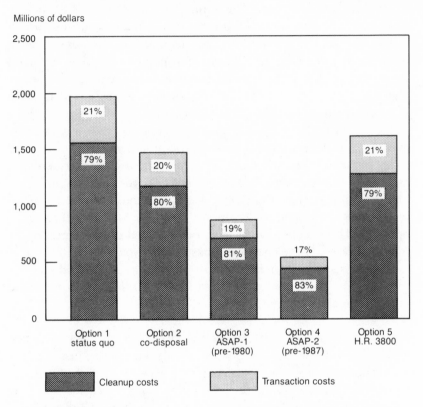

Millions of dollars

Source: RFF NPL Database, 1994.

from 17 percent under option 4 to 21 percent under both the status quo and H.R. 3800. The reason that transaction costs do not vary much relative to total responsible party expenditures is that all the savings in transaction costs occur at sites where cleanup responsibility is also shifted to the trust fund. In other words, although transaction costs fall at these sites, so too do the cleanup costs of responsible parties.

The other way to look at responsible party transaction costs is to view them as a percentage of total trust fund and responsible party site costs (figure 3-5). When looked at in this way, transaction costs decrease substantially under each liability alternative. Under the current liability scheme, we estimate transaction costs to be 16 percent of total annual site costs of $2.6 billion annually.[38] Transaction costs fall successively under options 2, 3, and 4 (to 12, 7, and 4 percent of site costs,

Figure 3-5. *Estimated Annual Responsible Party Cleanup and Transaction Costs as Compared to Total Site Costs under Five Options*

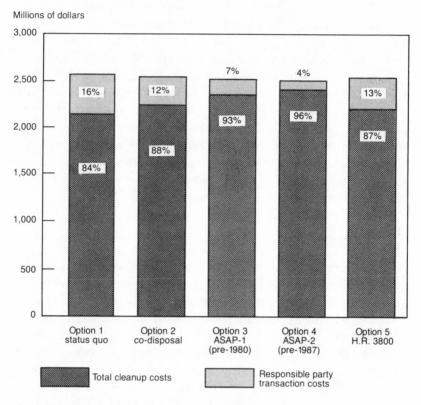

Millions of dollars

Source: RFF NPL Database, 1994.

respectively). The reason for the decrease is that under each of these alternatives more responsible parties are released from liability and responsibility for cleanup is transferred to the trust fund.

Responsible party transaction costs under option 5, although lower at 13 percent of site costs than under the status quo, are much higher than under the options that eliminate many sites from liability altogether. However, when transaction and cleanup costs are added together, as in figure 3-5, the absolute level of remaining costs of all five liability options is similar. This is because the savings in transaction costs that accrue as responsibility for cleanups is shifted to the trust fund are offset by the increase in cleanup costs when the federal government implements cleanups.

Not surprisingly, the distribution of private sector transaction costs mirrors the distribution of cleanup costs among industry categories, as shown in table 3-4. The chemical and allied products industry bears 23 percent of all responsible party transaction costs under all five liability options (this compares with approximately 25 percent of total cleanup costs). Although the distribution does not change much under each option, some industry sectors do see a real decrease in the actual dollars spent on transaction costs. For example, annual transaction costs for the chemical and allied products industry would be reduced from $97.6 million under the status quo to less than $70 million under option 2 and to $20.5 million under option 4. Again, the largest reduction in costs occurs under option 4—not surprising because the majority of cleanups would be implemented by the federal government under this approach, relieving responsible parties from most Superfund liability.

Effects on Responsible Parties

Our best estimates of the overall annual impacts on several industries of the cleanup and transaction costs likely to be incurred under the current and alternative sets of Superfund liability rules are presented in table 3-5. Having presented these estimated annual impacts, one question immediately suggests itself: Are these burdens manageable? That is, what effects will annual expenditures on the order of those presented in table 3-5 have on the industries in question? To this question we now turn. Before doing so, however, we would remind the reader of an important point made in chapter 1: because not all firms in an industry are encumbered by Superfund liability, cleanup and transaction costs are more likely to come out of corporate profits than they are to be recouped through higher product prices. For this reason the relevant comparisons are between annual cleanup and transaction costs on the one hand and profitability on the other.

For example, consider the mining industry. According to our estimates, the firms in this industry will incur cleanup and transaction costs of $220.5 million annually for the next ten years under the current Superfund liability standards. These liabilities would be reduced under any of the alternative liability approaches—by as much as $154.1 million (or 70 percent) under option 4, in which liability would be lifted for all wastes disposed of legally before 1987 at multiparty sites. Under the Clinton administration's proposal, the annual liability of the mining industry would be reduced by 36 percent to $140.3 million.

Table 3-4. *Estimated Annual Responsible Party Transaction Costs, by Industry Sector, under Five Options*[a]
Millions of dollars unless otherwise specified

Industry	Option 1 status quo	Option 2 co-disposal	Option 3 ASAP-1 (pre-1980)	Option 4 ASAP-2 (pre-1987)	Option 5 H.R. 3800[b]
Mining[c]	46.0 (11)	42.1 (14)	16.3 (10)	11.6 (13)	36.7 (11)
Lumber and wood products, except furniture[c]	21.8 (5)	20.0 (7)	8.5 (5)	5.0 (6)	17.4 (5)
Chemicals and allied products [c]	97.6 (23)	67.7 (23)	38.5 (23)	20.5 (23)	78.1 (23)
Petroleum refining and related industries[c]	22.0 (5)	12.0 (4)	8.2 (5)	4.0 (4)	17.5 (5)
Primary metals industries[c]	30.8 (7)	26.8 (9)	12.7 (8)	8.2 (9)	24.5 (7)
Fabricated metal products, except machinery and transportation equipment[c]	19.0 (5)	13.8 (5)	8.6 (5)	5.0 (5)	15.2 (5)
Electronic and other electrical equipment and components, except computer equipment[c]	12.4 (3)	9.8 (3)	5.8 (3)	3.0 (3)	10.0 (3)
All other manufacturing[c]	22.9 (5)	15.0 (5)	8.9 (5)	4.6 (5)	18.4 (6)
Miscellaneous[d]	23.1 (6)	14.5 (5)	9.8 (6)	5.4 (6)	18.5 (6)
Recycling[e]	53.9 (13)	48.4 (16)	22.9 (14)	8.8 (10)	42.8 (13)
Not attributed	68.9 (16)	27.6 (9)	25.7 (15)	14.6 (16)	54.7 (16)
Annual responsible party transaction cost[f]	418.5 (100)	297.7 (100)	165.9 (100)	90.6 (100)	333.8 (100)

Source: RFF NPL Database, 1994.
a. Numbers in parenthesees are percentages.
b. Responsible party transaction costs are calculated as percentages of total responsible party costs before EIRF reimbursement.
c. Industry sector based on Office of Management and Budget, *Standard Industrial Classification Manual* (Springfield, Va.: National Technical Information Service, 1987).
d. Includes all standard industrial classification (SIC) codes not specifically noted above, such as transportation, services, and public administration.
e. Category developed by Resources for the Future to classify activities not captured by the SIC; see appendix A.
f. Numbers may nor add because of rounding.

Table 3-5. *Estimated Total Annual Responsible Party Site Costs (Cleanup Costs plus Transaction Costs), by Industry Sector, under Five Options*
Millions of dollars

Industry	Option 1 status quo	Option 2 co-disposal	Option 3 ASAP-1 (pre-1980)	Option 4 ASAP-2 (pre-1987)	Option 5 H.R. 3800[a]
Mining[b]	220.5	202.5	89.5	66.4	140.3
Lumber and wood products, except furniture[b]	119.9	111.0	52.7	33.9	75.1
Chemicals and allied products[b]	492.0	363.8	226.2	140.2	307.7
Petroleum refining and related industries[b]	97.4	56.5	38.9	21.1	60.7
Primary metals industries[b]	148.8	131.7	68.3	46.4	96.1
Fabricated metal products, except machinery and transportation equipment[b]	98.7	76.5	51.0	32.8	63.6
Electronic and other electrical equipment and components, except computer equipment[b]	70.1	58.5	38.0	23.5	44.6
All other manufacturing[b]	117.6	83.9	54.0	32.4	73.4
Miscellaneous[c]	114.5	78.7	55.7	34.0	72.7
Recycling[d]	211.8	189.7	92.1	37.2	130.7
Not attributed	286.2	118.2	111.2	65.8	180.1
Total annual responsible party cost[e]	1,977.5	1,470.8	877.7	533.6	1,244.9

Source: RFF NPL Database, 1994.
a. Responsible party transaction costs are calculated as percentages of total responsible party costs before EIRF reimbursement.
b. Industry sector based on Office of Management and Budget, *Standard Industrial Classification Manual* (Springfield, Va.: National Technical Information Service, 1987).
c. Includes all standard industrial classification (SIC) codes not specifically noted above, such as transportation, services, and public administration.
d. Category developed by Resources for the Future to classify activities not captured by the SIC; see appendix A.
e. Numbers may not add because of rounding.

How do these figures compare to profitability in the mining industry? The answer is startling. In 1991 before-tax profits for the mining industry amounted to only $300 million. After taxes in 1991 the industry reported losses of $300 million. Even in 1990, a much better year for the industry, after-tax profits amounted to only $1 billion.[39] Thus the annual cleanup and transaction cost liabilities we estimate for the mining industry—for the 1,134 nonfederal sites on the current

NPL—represent a significant share of mining industry profits. These liabilities would make matters even more difficult for companies in the industry should future years result in after-tax losses like those of 1991 (or like those of 1985, when after-tax losses in the industry amounted to $6.1 billion). Another way to say this is that any of the proposed changes in Superfund liability standards would make a significant difference to the mining industry, given the magnitude of its cleanup and transaction costs in relation to its profitability.

But it can be argued that expected costs under current Superfund liability rules are already reflected in the prices of the shares of mining firms. The share-price reductions depend on the extent to which potential investors already know about the number of Superfund sites to be cleaned up by responsible parties. Any reduction in Superfund liability would then provide unexpected capital gains to new buyers of these shares.

The situation looks different when we examine the chemical industry. In absolute terms, the annual cleanup and transaction costs that would be incurred by firms in the industry over the next decade are larger than those of the mining industry. Depending on the option under consideration, the chemical industry would spend almost two to three times as much as the mining industry each year. At first blush, then, it might appear that the chemical industry would be taking a harder hit.

But after-tax profits for the chemical industry are in much better shape than they are in mining. For instance, in 1991 the chemical industry reported after-tax profits of $21 billion, more than sixty times the profit in the mining industry.[40] According to chemical industry data, after-tax profits were expected to increase to about $24 billion in 1992, second only to 1989, when they were $24.5 billion.[41] Although estimated Superfund cleanup and transaction cost liabilities would be significant for the industry in absolute terms, relative to the after-tax profits that we believe are the relevant basis for comparison, these liabilities are not nearly so burdensome as for the mining industry.

What about the petroleum refining industry? Although strictly comparable data are lacking for this industry, we do know that twenty of the leading firms in the industry (including the very largest) had net income in 1991 (analogous to after-tax profits) of $13.2 billion, down from $16.7 billion in 1990.[42] Thus our estimate of that industry's annual liability under option 1 (the status quo)—$97.4 million—is less than 1 percent of the annual net income (or profits) of the twenty leading firms. From 1982 to 1991, income for these twenty firms averaged $14.4 billion a year.

Lest there be any confusion, this is not to trivialize the cleanup and transaction costs for the petroleum industry. The difference between the current liability standards (option 1) and the least onerous alternative to the industry (option 4) amounts to $76.3 million annually. All other things being equal, this is money the industry would be happy either to pass on to shareholders or to retain as earnings to be used for new exploration, capital investment, or other purposes. Nevertheless, it is important to view these liabilities in relation to industry profitability (or that of its leading firms), and in this context the relative sums involved are not very large.

The primary metals industry also bears substantial cleanup and transaction cost liability (see table 3-5). We estimate that the industry would incur annual cleanup and transaction costs ranging from $46.4 million under option 4 to nearly $150 million under option 1. Annual profits in the industry averaged $1.4 billion from 1983 to 1992 but were higher—averaging $3.3 billion annually—from 1988 to 1992.[43] Thus under option 1 our estimate of cleanup and transaction costs liability amounts to about 11 percent of industry profitability as averaged over a recent ten-year period, and to about 4.5 percent of annual profits over the most recent five-year period for which data are available. This puts the primary metals industry somewhere between the mining industry and the chemical industry in terms of estimated liabilities relative to profits.

We also forecast substantial cleanup and transaction cost liabilities for the lumber and wood products sector. However, a good bit of this liability would fall upon small, privately owned wood-treating companies, for which there are few data pertaining to profitability. Thus we have resisted making liability-to-profitability estimates for this sector.

Although Superfund liability is best compared to profits in each industry, data on profits are not always available. For another comparison, we can indicate the size of each industry by using data on value added from the input-output model described in chapter 4. Liability under current Superfund rules, as shown in table 3-5, would then constitute the percentages of value added shown in table 3-6.

Two brief caveats to this discussion about cleanup liabilities. First, suppose annual liabilities in a particular industry are small in relation to annual profitability, as we estimate to be the case for chemicals or petroleum refining. Does this mean that each of the companies in the industry is immune to economic harm? Most certainly not. There will no doubt be

Table 3-6. *Industry Liability as Percentage of Value Added*

Industry	Estimated current annual liability (millions of dollars)	Value added in 1990 (billions of dollars)	Liability as percent of value added
Mining	220.5	32.2	0.7
Lumber and wood products, except furniture	119.9	25.8	0.5
Chemicals and allied products	492.0	126.7	0.4
Petroleum refining and related industries	97.4	37.6	0.3
Primary metals industries	148.8	47.3	0.3
Fabricated metal products, except machinery and transportation equipment	98.7	71.8	0.1
Electronic and other electrical equipment and components, except computer equipment	70.1	93.7	0.1

Sources: For first column, RFF NPL Database, 1994. For second column, authors' calculations based on data from "Benchmark Input-Output Accounts for the U.S. Economy, 1987," *Survey of Current Business*, vol. 74 (April 1994), pp. 73–115; Robert E. Yuskavage, "Gross Product by Industry, 1988–91," *Survey of Current Business*, vol. 73 (November 1993), pp. 33–44.

certain ones, including some with well-known names, for whom cleanup and transaction costs would be an uncomfortably large share of (or perhaps even exceed) earnings. It will be small solace to these firms to know that, on average, the industry of which they are a part seems capable of digesting Superfund liability without severe adverse economic effects. This would be especially true for companies whose Superfund liability threatens dividend payments, significantly reduces share value, makes it difficult to raise new capital, or may threaten bankruptcy. Even a healthy forest can contain sick or dying trees.

Second, underlying our comparisons of annual cleanup liabilities and transaction costs on the one hand and annual profitability on the other is the presumption that none of the cleanup and transaction costs would be passed forward in higher product prices. This is the most reasonable assumption to make, but there would be exceptions. In certain submarkets within some industries, barriers to entry would inevitably give some firms the ability to pass forward some of their cleanup and transaction costs. In other words, the markets for each and every good produced by the industries considered here are not perfectly competitive. Thus some market power will mean some forward shifting not unlike that described in chapter 4. However, we are comfortable with the assumption that shareholders of the companies affected would bear the brunt of cleanup and transaction cost liability.

CHAPTER FOUR

Taxes for Superfund

THE DESIGNING of good tax policy is often stymied by trade-offs that must be made among competing objectives. It may be difficult for one tax to achieve multiple goals simultaneously, including, in the case of Superfund, goals to collect certain revenue, minimize administrative cost (of the Internal Revenue Service in collecting the tax), minimize compliance cost (of taxpayers in filling out forms), minimize interference with economic efficiency (of private resource allocation decisions), and be fair (perhaps by several definitions).

In this chapter we describe three major taxes that provide Superfund's trust fund revenues—the crude petroleum tax, chemical feedstocks tax, and environmental income tax (EIT). These and other proposed Superfund taxes are then evaluated with respect to the multiple goals of good tax policy, starting with a discussion of administrative and compliance costs and why Superfund taxes score particularly low on the compliance cost criterion. Compliance costs are seen to be a relatively high fraction of, and in the case of the EIT may even exceed, the revenue collected.

In subsequent sections we discuss economic efficiency—the extent to which a tax may interfere with otherwise efficient decisions of taxpayers about how much to buy of a taxed input or how much to produce of a taxed output—alternative concepts of equity and the extent to which each Superfund tax fits each concept, and who bears the burden of Superfund taxes. Some Superfund taxes apply to petroleum and chemicals used in production, but firms that buy those taxed inputs may be able to raise the prices of their products and thus shift the burden onto others. The economic incidence of the tax can only be assessed by estimating final product prices.

Toward that end we apply an input-output model of the U.S. economy that includes information on all the commodities used as inputs in the production of each output. When those inputs are taxed, and when each industry can cover those costs in equilibrium by raising the price of its own output, the ultimate effect on the price of each output can be calculated. Thus we use the model to estimate the ways in which Superfund tax burdens get spread across the economy.

Recent proposals for new Superfund taxes are then evaluated with respect to the criteria for good tax policy given above; we use the input-output model to calculate their effects on output prices. A concluding section discusses some of the implications of these analyses for tax policymaking.

Existing Superfund Taxes

Taxes on crude petroleum and chemicals, and corporations' alternative minimum taxable income (AMTI) in excess of $2 million (the corporate environmental income tax) are the three major taxes providing trust fund revenues. The petroleum and chemicals subject to tax are not final products for sale to consumers, but intermediate goods for use in producing some other final product. The taxes apply to the use of these intermediate inputs whether they are purchased from another firm or produced within the same firm. Imports are taxed, exports are exempt. In general the chemical and petroleum taxes are levied on specific goods thought to contain hazardous substances. The environmental income tax was added in 1986 when the Comprehensive Environmental Response, Liability, and Compensation Act (CERCLA), which established Superfund in 1980, was amended by the Superfund Amendments and Reauthorization Act (SARA), and may reflect concern that hazardous substances are present in a broad range of goods used by firms not in the chemical and petroleum sectors. Since 1986 the EIT has become a major source of additional trust fund revenue.

The tax liabilities for each of the three tax categories for 1987 through 1991 are presented in table 4-1. As shown in figure 2-1, chapter 2, additional trust fund moneys derive from general revenues, interest on the fund, and cost recovery actions.

Table 4-1. *Superfund Tax Liabilities, 1987–91*
Millions of dollars unless otherwise specified

	Tax					
Subject of tax	1987	1988	1989	1990	1991	Total
Petroleum						
Domestic	258.0	250.1	237.0	278.8	290.4	1,314.3
Imported	270.5	297.5	333.1	266.4	259.7	1,427.2
Subtotal	528.5	547.6	570.1	545.2	550.1	2,741.5
Percent of total						
Superfund taxes	45.8	41.2	43.2	40.1	41.4	42.2
Chemical feedstocks						
Organic	224.8	241.3	219.5	236.8	237.3	1,159.7
Inorganic	48.5	53.0	50.0	49.4	50.4	251.3
Subtotal	273.3	294.3	269.5	286.2	287.7	1,411.0
Percent of total						
Superfund taxes	23.7	22.1	20.4	21.0	21.6	21.7
Imported chemical						
substances	. . .	. . .	7.8	9.7	11.9	29.4
Percent of total						
Superfund taxes	. . .	. . .	0.6	0.7	0.9	0.5
Environmental income						
tax (EIT)	351.3	487.9	471.8	520.2	479.3	2,310.5
Percent of total						
Superfund taxes	30.5	36.7	35.8	38.2	36.1	35.6
Total	1,153.1	1,329.8	1,319.2	1,361.3	1,329.0	6,492.4

Sources: For the petroleum tax, Internal Revenue Service, *Statistics of Income*, environmental tax statistics (Treasury Department, various issues) (excludes petroleum tax for the Oil Spill Liability Trust Fund); for the chemical feedstock tax, Charlotte Dougherty and Elizabeth Gilson, "Economic Impacts of Superfund Taxes," prepared by Industrial Economics, Inc., for the Office of Policy Analysis, U.S. Environmental Protection Agency, February, 1994, exhibit 3-3; for the imported chemical substances tax, Dougherty and Gilson, "Economic Impacts of Superfund Taxes," exhibit 2-2; for the EIT, Internal Revenue Service, *Statistics of Income*, corporate income tax returns (Treasury Department, various issues).

Petroleum Tax

Under Superfund, an oil refiner is required to pay tax when crude oil is received at a U.S. refinery. An importer must also pay the tax when crude oil and refined petroleum products enter the United States. Until 1985 (under CERCLA) both the refiner and the importer paid 0.79 cents a barrel of petroleum.[1] The 1986 amendments to Superfund multiplied this rate tenfold to 8.2 cents a barrel for the refiner and 11.7 cents a barrel for the importer. In January 1989, because of the General Agreement on Tariffs and Trade (GATT), the rates were changed for both the refiner and the importer to 9.7 cents a barrel.

Table 4-1 shows the Superfund tax liabilities for domestic and imported oil for 1987–91; the subtotal shows the sum of these taxes. For the period shown, the petroleum tax contributed from 40 to 46 percent of total Superfund taxes.

Chemical Taxes

Chemical taxes apply to both domestic and imported chemical feedstocks. The chemical taxes are levied on the sale or use of forty-two organic and inorganic chemical feedstocks and on at least seventy-three imported chemical substances (to the extent that they were produced overseas using chemical feedstocks that would have been taxed in the United States).

When CERCLA was passed in 1980, the tax rates were originally set at $4.87 a ton for organic chemicals and at similar rates for inorganic chemicals.[2] When Superfund was amended by SARA in 1986, the tax rates were revised for some chemicals. For example, the rate for xylene was raised temporarily to $10.13 a ton. The chemical tax liabilities for 1987–91 are presented in table 4-1; during this period the chemical feedstocks tax contributed from 20 to 24 percent of total Superfund taxes.

SARA also levied a tax on fifty imported chemical substances. Since the 1986 amendments, at least twenty-three more have been added to the list subject to the Superfund tax. Taxes on these substances are meant to reflect the tax that would have been paid on the chemical feedstocks used in their production.[3] Tax liabilities on chemical imports for 1989–91 are shown in table 4-1. This tax contributed less than 1 percent of total Superfund taxes.[4]

Environmental Income Tax

The Superfund Amendments and Reauthorization Act levies a tax of 0.12 percent on every corporation's modified alternative minimum taxable income (AMTI) in excess of $2 million, regardless of whether that firm is subject to the alternative minimum tax (AMT).[5] The firm's AMTI is modified to remove deductions for net operating losses and for the environmental income tax itself. Since the EIT was added in 1986 it has become an increasingly important source of Superfund financing. In 1990 the EIT was generating 38 percent of total Superfund taxes (table 4-1).

The petroleum tax rate ($.097 a barrel) and chemical tax rates (such as $4.87 a ton) do not change with inflation. Collections from these taxes grow only as the economy uses more oil and chemicals. In contrast, the environmental income tax is based on a measure of profits that increases both with inflation and with real economic growth. For this reason, it may continue to provide an increasing percentage of Superfund tax revenues.

Administrative and Compliance Costs

Minimizing the cost of collecting revenue is an important goal of tax policy. The entire budget of the Internal Revenue Service is about $6 billion a year, including rent, equipment, and the salaries of clerks, auditors, and lawyers. This administrative cost is less than 0.6 percent of federal tax revenue, which now exceeds $1 trillion. Thus the United States is fairly efficient at collecting taxes. The IRS does not reveal what portion of its administrative costs are associated with each Superfund tax.

The U.S government has a relatively low collection cost because it puts most of the cost on the taxpayers themselves. The compliance cost to taxpayers includes not only the dollars paid to accountants and lawyers, but also the value of all taxpayers' time spent collecting receipts, reading instructions, and filling out forms. For the individual income tax, Joel Slemrod and Nikki Sorum estimated that in 1982 "between 1.8 and 2.1 billion hours of taxpayer time were spent on filing tax returns, and between $3.0 billion and $3.4 billion was spent on professional tax assistance."[6] Slemrod and Sorum valued the taxpayers' time at their net wage rate and found that the total compliance cost was 5 to 7 percent of revenue. Thus the compliance cost associated with the individual income tax was ten times the administrative cost to the Internal Revenue Service.

Both logic and evidence suggest that many of these administrative and compliance costs are fixed costs of calculating the tax base, not marginal costs of collecting more revenue by raising the rate of tax on a given tax base. Compliance cost depends on the complexity and number of forms to be filed by taxpayers, just as administrative costs depend on the number of forms to be checked by the IRS. Under the income tax, different forms are required for itemized deductions, depreciation calculations, and each type of income such as interest, dividends, capital gains, rents, and self-employment earnings. The last step in the process is multiplying the total tax base by a tax rate, or looking up the tax in a table provided by the IRS—a step that is equally simple whether the tax rate is 1 percent or 30 percent. Thus the technology of tax collections exhibits economies of scale. Administrative cost or compliance cost as a fraction of tax revenue can be expected to fall as the tax rate and revenue become larger.

The same economies hold for excise taxes. For example, Cedrick Sandford, Michael Godwin, and Peter Hardwick found that when the United Kingdom increased the value added tax (VAT) rate from 8 to 15 percent in 1979, "over the next few years the [administrative] cost:revenue ratio in the collection of VAT fell from 2 percent to one percent mainly, though not solely, because of the increase in rate."[7] They found further evidence of economies of scale by looking at firms of different sizes. For 1986–87 in the United Kingdom, the cost of complying with the VAT as a percentage of the tax base was smaller for businesses that were larger, as measured either by the tax base or by the number of employees.[8] Similar results have been found in regard to goods and services tax (GST) in Canada and the corporate income tax in the United States.[9] Although a scale economy of this kind pertains to firm size rather than tax rate, the implication is that compliance cost includes a fixed annual amount that depends on the number and complexity of forms used to calculate the tax base.

This analysis suggests that the most efficient way to collect revenue for Superfund would be to increase slightly any existing excise tax rate, the corporate income tax rate, or even personal income tax rates. If Superfund had introduced only one special tax, the revenue would have been collected most efficiently with a single tax rate on a relatively simple tax base. But Superfund introduced several special taxes with different rates. The petroleum tax is levied on oil firms at only 9.7 cents a barrel; the chemical feedstocks tax is levied on a different set of firms, at many different rates, on eleven different organic chemicals, thirty-one inorganic chemicals, and at least seventy-three imported chemical substances. Enforcement must require a degree in chemistry. Yet all these Superfund excise taxes together brought in only $841 million in 1990, less than one-tenth of 1 percent of total federal tax revenue. There are no direct estimates of administrative or compliance costs for these Superfund taxes, but the costs must be a high fraction of this minor amount of revenue.

In regard to Superfund's corporate environmental income tax, compliance is even more complicated. EIT calculation starts with the alternative minimum tax. To its regular taxable income, the firm must add back net operating loss deductions, "adjustments," and "preference" items such as interest from certain tax-exempt bonds. Adjustments include the difference between depreciation according to regular tax schedules and depreciation according to AMT rules. Thus for each asset it purchases, the firm must keep track of one depreciation schedule for book purposes, another for the regular tax, and a third for the AMT. The firm must also add back some deductions for mining costs, intangible drilling costs, and pollution control facilities.[10] Then the alternative minimum tax requires an additional calculation of profits, termed adjusted current earnings. The tentative minimum tax is 20 percent of alternative minimum taxable income (AMTI), and the firm pays an alternative minimum tax equal to the excess of the tentative minimum tax over the regular tax, if any.

Regardless of whether the firm pays AMT, the Superfund's EIT applies at a 0.12 percent rate to "modified" AMTI in excess of $2 million, where AMTI is modified to disallow deductions for the EIT and for net operating losses.

If all firms had to calculate AMTI anyway, the environmental income tax would not introduce much additional compliance cost. Of the 12,199 firms that paid the EIT in 1990, however, 8,584 (70 percent) did not pay an alternative minimum tax.[11] The additional cost to such firms of complying with the EIT could be substantial if it is anything like the cost of complying with the AMT as estimated by Joel Slemrod and Marsha Blumenthal. They surveyed 365 large corporations and found that the average cost of their corporate income tax compliance in 1990 was $1.57 million. Using regression analysis to determine the effect of certain firm characteristics on compliance cost, Slemrod and Blumenthal also found that "being subject to the alternative minimum tax (AMT) adds 16.9 percent; this is true even though all but three of the firms report that they must *calculate* the alternative minimum tax liability. This result implies that those firms that suspect that they will actually have AMT liability devote more resources to its calculation and planning implications."[12]

In other words, even though almost all firms incurred some additional compliance cost just to determine whether they were subject to the alternative minimum tax, the extra 16.9 percent of compliance cost was incurred only by firms that really were subject to the AMT. The additional compliance cost was 16.9 percent of $1.57 million, or $265,330 for each firm. We use this figure later to provide rough estimates of EIT compliance costs.

Because of its size, however, the figure raises four questions that bear further discussion. First, are Slemrod and Blumenthal's estimates believable? The $1.57 million compliance cost seems large, but the authors looked only at very large firms (98 of their 365 firms are in the Fortune 500 list of the largest in the United States). The estimated compliance cost was only 3 percent of the taxes paid by these firms. Thus it seems a reasonable expenditure. Second, could alternative minimum tax calculations cost 17 percent more? This figure seems low, since the AMT is a parallel tax system that essentially doubles the number of calculations necessary to obtain taxable income, allowable deductions, and tax due. Thus $265,330 is a believable estimate of the cost of AMT compliance for these firms.

Third, does the cost of AMT compliance indicate the cost of EIT compliance? Because all large firms perform rough calculations to determine AMT liability, $265,330 represents the incremental cost of actually having to pay the alternative minimum tax. The same increment should apply to the cost of having to pay the environmental income tax, if calculations are performed properly, since the same tax base is used for both. But compliance cost includes tax planning costs, which may increase with the tax rate. Firms may expend more effort to reduce AMT at the 20 percent rate than to reduce EIT at the 0.12 percent rate.

Fourth, are the firms in Slemrod and Blumenthal's study representative of firms that pay the environmental income tax? The surveyed firms were large, but so are firms that pay EIT; EIT applies only to the extent that alternative minimum taxable income exceeds $2 million. Of 3.7 million corporate tax returns in 1990, the IRS reported that only 5,589 (0.15 percent) were for "giants," firms with more than $250 million in assets. Of 32,462 firms that paid AMT in 1990, however, 1,324 (4 percent) were giants. Even more striking is that 3,131 of the 12,199 firms that paid EIT in 1990—26 percent—were giants.[13]

We conclude that $265,330 is a reasonable estimate of the EIT compliance cost of firms that did not pay an alternative minimum tax in 1990, and we use that figure to provide rough estimates of total EIT compliance cost. If that compliance cost applied to all 8,584 firms that had to pay EIT even though they did not have to pay AMT, the additional compliance cost for the environmental income tax was $2.278 billion. This calculation ignores compliance cost for EIT firms that were already subject to the alternative minimum tax. The total revenue from the environmental income tax in 1990 was $520.2 million (table 4-1); thus the ratio of estimated compliance cost to revenue for the EIT in 1990 was 4.38. The Superfund EIT tax may impose on firms compliance costs that are more than four times the revenue collected.[14]

It must be kept in mind, however, that Slemrod and Blumenthal's estimates pertained to very large companies. Of the 8,584 firms that paid the environmental income tax but not the alternative minimum tax, the IRS reported that 1,952 (23 percent) were giants. If the $265,330 cost is applied only to these 1,952 giants, the total compliance cost would be $518 million, which is 100 percent of total EIT revenue in 1990. This last calculation ignores compliance cost for the 10,247 firms that were not giants or that had already paid AMT. We think this last calculation is a lower bound.[15] Thus compliance cost may be at least 100 percent of EIT revenue, and possibly four times revenue.

Several implications of this analysis bear comment. First, the environmental income tax does not make sense. Much pain could be saved by using a slightly higher rate for any other tax instrument because new calculations would not be required. Second, if political considerations dictate that the EIT must be retained, any new Superfund taxes should clearly be avoided. If the rate of the environmental income tax were doubled, revenue would double without any increase in compliance cost; the ratio of compliance cost to revenue would be cut in half. Third, extra revenue should not be obtained by lowering the $2 million AMTI threshold. Such a change would subject many smaller firms to unnecessary calculations without raising much revenue.

Economic Efficiency

The goal of economic efficiency is to minimize the excess burden that arises when loss to the economy is larger than revenue received by the government. The problem arises because producers might use less of a taxed input and consumers might buy less of a taxed output. These changes in behavior interfere with the private market's ability to allocate resources to their most productive uses. Excess burden is the cost to the economy when taxpayers decide to do without some of the taxed commodity, or to use a less desired substitute.

The concept of excess burden is illustrated in figure 4-1, where for any good for final consumption there are a downward-sloping demand curve and a flat supply curve (given by the marginal cost of production).

Figure 4-1. *Tax Burden plus Excess Burden Borne by Consumers*

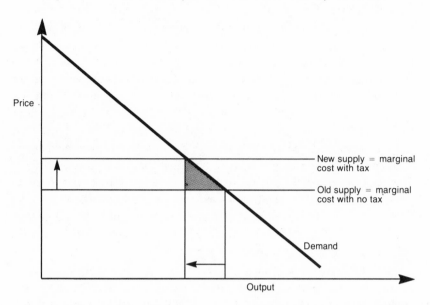

Initially, for this diagram we assume no monopoly power or externalities such as pollution. With no fixed costs and with perfect competition, the equilibrium price (at the intersection of the demand curve and the supply curve) just equals the break-even price (enough to cover the cost of producing each good with a normal return, but no excess profits). With a tax, the price rises and the quantity falls. Even though the firm might be required by law to pay the tax, the burden is shifted completely to consumers in the form of higher prices.[16] Tax revenue is the tax rate times the new quantity.

In figure 4-1, consumers lose not only the tax revenue (by paying the higher price on the new quantity) but also the area of the shaded triangle. This area represents excess burden, the dollar value of the inconvenience of cutting back on the number of units purchased.[17]

Economists have used this kind of model to measure excess burden for many different taxes. This economic loss—the area of the triangle—depends directly on the slope of the demand curve or the elasticity of demand. If the demand curve is steep, for example, price has a small effect on quantity and excess burden is small. Thus the measure of excess burden would depend on estimates of the original cost of production, the size of the tax rate, and the elasticity of demand.

We do not attempt in this book to estimate the excess burden of Superfund taxes for several reasons. First, there are no estimates of the elasticity of demand for individual commodities such as organic or inorganic chemicals. However, such demand elasticities are not necessary for our calculations of price effects later in this chapter. In our input-output model, as in figure 4-1, prices are determined completely by the location of the flat marginal cost curve. Therefore we can calculate the old price from the cost of production with no taxes, and the new price from the cost of production with taxes on some inputs, for each industry output considered. We can calculate price changes without the demand elasticities, but we cannot calculate quantity changes or excess burdens.

A second reason for not estimating the excess burden of Superfund taxes is that typical measures of excess burden would be small. An illustrative calculation suggests that these costs might be only 1 percent of revenue.[18] Compared to compliance cost, estimated earlier to exceed 100 percent of revenue, excess burden is small.

A third (and most important) reason is that our analysis of excess burden pertains only to a market that has no other taxes or distortions such as monopoly power or pollution. If such distortions are important, then estimates of excess burden that ignore them could err by many orders of magnitude. The intuition for this problem is straightforward. Suppose, for example, that the price of a gallon of gasoline is raised 2 percent by existing taxes and then another 2 percent by the Superfund tax on petroleum. Consumers who had already suffered some inconvenience by cutting back after the first increase would have to proceed to more drastic means of reducing consumption after the second. If the tax in figure 4-1 were doubled to reflect the additional tax, the geometry indicates that the size of the excess burden triangle would be quadrupled.

The existence of these other distortions would mean that the market was operating inefficiently before the Superfund tax was imposed. If the quantity of a taxed commodity was already too small because of preexisting taxes or monopoly power that raised the price, any further price hike would impose disproportionately more burden on consumers. Conversely, if the quantity was already too large because of associated pollution, a tax could reduce quantity toward the lower socially efficient level. In this case excess burden of the tax could be negative. Without having adequate estimates of these other distortions, it is not possible to determine the size of the excess burden of Superfund taxes or even whether it will have a plus or a minus sign.

Chemical feedstocks tax rates were originally set in response to certain pollutants found at Superfund sites. Taxes on these chemical inputs must be paid regardless of how a plant disposes of hazardous by-products, however, so the taxes provide no direct incentive to reduce pollution. The direct effect of a tax on chemicals is only to discourage use of the taxed chemicals. But these chemicals are goods that are helpful in the production of other goods. We conclude therefore that Superfund taxes for the most part are not used as incentives to achieve economic efficiency. The intent of CERCLA and SARA is not to discourage the use of helpful chemical inputs, or even to discourage pollution; the primary intent is to raise revenue with some attention to fairness.

Concepts of Equity

One concept of tax equity is the ability-to-pay principle, according to which taxes should be collected on the basis of income, wealth, or some other measure of ability to pay taxes. The personal income tax operates on this principle, with higher rates applied to those with higher incomes. This principle could easily be applied under CERCLA, as it would merely suggest that Superfund taxes should be collected from those with higher incomes. Superfund revenues might thus be raised by using additional personal income taxes.

Instead, CERCLA tries to follow another concept of equity known as the polluter pays principle. CERCLA attempts first to use liability standards to collect from the specific firms, government agencies, or individuals held responsible for contamination at specific sites. (As noted earlier Superfund liability also attaches to owners and operators of contaminated sites who may not have actually caused the contamination.) Even for the tax portion of its financing, Superfund attempts to collect from those most likely to have contributed to the problem, if only indirectly. The chemical feedstocks and petroleum taxes were apportioned originally on the basis of a survey of the chemical composition of hazardous waste sites.[19] The relationship is rough, however. Congress set the same tax rate for all organic chemicals, exempted three inorganic chemicals (lead, phosphoric acid, and antimony sulfide), and switched zinc chloride and zinc sulfate for zinc and zinc oxide. Congress increased the petroleum tax tenfold in 1986, but not on the basis of new information about substances at Superfund sites. The environmental income tax is not designed to target specific generators of waste.

Generally, the polluter pays principle works hand-in-hand with the goal of economic efficiency. If a polluting firm is required to pay a tax (or buy a permit) for every unit of pollution emitted, then the firm faces the right incentives to cut back the amount of pollution. Such a tax has no excess burden, but it does have a social gain from discouraging pollution. These principles work together properly only when the tax is imposed at the time of the pollution, however. Unfortunately, that is not the case under CERCLA. In many instances contamination of sites took place before CERCLA was passed in 1980, so those whose actions caused the contamination had no incentive to avoid polluting at the time. Superfund taxes imposed now, after the fact, can play no role in discouraging past pollution.[20]

This discrepancy has even wider implications for the logic of the polluter pays principle. Firms may have used waste management practices that were acceptable at the time of disposal, even though their practices did not cover full environmental costs. In other words, production costs were lower than social costs. Because many small firms operated in each industry, however, competition would tend to drive output prices down to the level of production cost: anybody trying to charge more than the normal production cost would lose business to another firm charging less.[21] As a consequence, consumers received the benefit of those low-cost waste management practices. Shareholders received only a normal rate of return, so they did not benefit from polluting.[22]

These considerations bring us to a third concept of equity, the beneficiary pays principle.[23] This principle suggests that because consumers benefit from low-cost waste management practices, the cost of cleanup should be recouped with a tax on consumers. As figure 4-1 shows, with competition and constant marginal costs, a tax on each unit output is expected to be passed forward to consumers. However, the problem remains that the individuals who currently consume these products are probably not the same ones who took the benefit through earlier consumption of the products.

Using these principles of equity, we can now compare the equity of CERCLA's liability rules with tax financing. Because liability under CERCLA is retroactive, when a new Superfund site is discovered, a firm may be forced to bear costs that were not expected. For the most part these costs cannot be passed on to consumers because the firm competes with other firms (or with potential entrants into the industry) that may not face the extra costs. As a consequence, most of the burden of retroactive liability is likely to fall on current shareholders. Because corporate shares change hands rapidly, retroactive liability places the burden on many who did not own shares at the time the pollution took place. To the extent that retroactive liability collects from new shareholders rather than from the former managers or shareholders who were responsible for the pollution, it does not really follow the polluter pays principle. And to the extent that it collects from shareholders rather than from consumers, retroactive liability does not follow the beneficiary pays principle either.

Similarly, tax financing collects from consumers rather than from managers or shareholders who were responsible for past pollution. And many consumers must not be the same ones who previously took the benefit of low prices that did not cover the full social cost of pollution. Thus tax financing as well follows neither the polluter pays principle nor the beneficiary pays principle.

Only if the same individuals have owned the firm since pollution began does retroactive liability burden the shareholders who were responsible, but even those shareholders did not benefit from earlier low-cost waste management practices. They earned normal returns, according to this theory, while consumers took the benefit. And only if the same individuals are now buying the firm's products do Superfund taxes burden the consumers who took the benefit. Otherwise, Superfund leaves a windfall gain to earlier consumers who paid low prices for goods that were produced too cheaply, and imposes a windfall loss on new shareholders who paid a normal price for shares of a firm that did not expect the discovery of a Superfund site.

Because Superfund cannot follow exactly either the polluter pays principle or the beneficiary pays principle, perhaps it should give up the attempt to do so. One implication of this is that reform could follow the ability-to-pay principle by collecting a bit more personal income tax. Such a reform would save considerable administrative and compliance costs as well, as discussed earlier. The federal government could still sue unscrupulous firms that earned illicit profits by knowingly and negligently polluting the environment.

Effects on Prices

Congress can decide who is legally liable to pay a tax, but it cannot legislate the ultimate distribution of the tax burden. A tax on one good may reverberate through the economy in such a way that prices of other goods are affected. An untaxed good may end up with a higher price, and anyone who buys it bears a burden.[24]

In this section we use the input-output model to account for some of these indirect effects. The model uses information on each industry's purchase of intermediate inputs that are produced by other industries. The cost of producing each output then depends on the gross-of-tax cost of buying all the inputs.[25] We first describe the model in general terms, then examine the assumptions necessary for the model and calculate the price changes attributable to existing Superfund taxes. A detailed description of the model can be found in appendix C.

The Input-Output Model

CERCLA and SARA impose taxes on the purchase or use of chemical feedstocks and crude petroleum. They also impose a tax on a measure of corporate income, or return to capital. Returns to labor and capital are components of value added because the term is defined as sales revenue minus the cost of intermediate inputs. All these taxes raise the cost of production. We assume here that in any particular industry all firms face the same increase in cost of production. As they respond by raising their own output prices, their customers may cut back on purchases. Some firms may suffer losses in the short run and eventually may have to cut production or exit the industry. After the dust settles, remaining firms can sell the reduced output at a higher price that just covers the new higher cost of production. Under competitive conditions the output price rises by exactly the increase in cost.[26] The remaining empirical problem is to determine the extent to which each price rises, that is, each industry's use of taxed inputs such as chemical feedstocks and petroleum.

The U.S. Department of Commerce provides information on the use of all (taxed and untaxed) inputs, in matrix form, for 480 industries.[27] The most recent complete input-output data are for 1987, but we scale these amounts to 1990 for each industry using the ratio of GDP in 1990 to GDP in 1987. A column of this matrix shows, for a particular industry, the amount of each of the other 479 outputs that is used as an input.[28] For this study fewer categories suffice, so we aggregate the 480 industries into 41 categories (table 4-2).[29] In table 4-2 our identification numbers for those categories appear in column 1, and the standard industrial classification (SIC) number appears in column 2. We start with industries at the two-digit SIC level, then we make adjustments, keeping the two-digit level for most manufacturing industries (SIC numbers 20 through 39) but separating wood preserving from other lumber and wood products (because wood preserving is involved in a number of sites on the National Priorities List).[30] Chemicals are separated into three categories that are taxed at different rates (organic chemicals, inorganic chemicals, and untaxed chemicals). We collapse nonmanufacturing industries into fewer categories; two industries are used to represent agriculture, and one industry each is used to represent construction, transportation, wholesale trade, retail trade, finance, and services.[31]

Although we do not show the whole matrix, its numbers confirm general expectations. The output of crude petroleum and natural gas (our no. 5) is a major input for petroleum refining (no. 20), for example, and the output of refined petroleum is a major input for petroleum related products (no. 21) and transportation (no. 32).[32] In previously published matrices, for 1982 and earlier, refined petroleum and related products were also important inputs for organic chemicals (no. 18, sometimes called petrochemicals), but 1987 data reveal that organic chemicals are now produced in the United States more from other imported organic chemicals and less directly from refined petroleum. Both organic (no. 18) and inorganic chemicals (no. 17) are inputs for the other (untaxed) chemical industry (no. 19), and are also major inputs for textile mill products (no. 10) and wood preserving (no. 13).

Table 4-2, column 3, shows the effective rates of tax, under current Superfund laws, on the intermediate use of crude petroleum, inorganic chemicals, and organic chemicals.[33] The petroleum tax applies to all purchases of crude petroleum. Unfortunately, even the most detailed input-output data use only one industry to represent crude petroleum and natural gas (no. 5), and its output is purchased by both refineries and utilities. Virtually all of the crude oil is purchased by refineries (no. 20), however; whereas natural gas is purchased by gas distribution utilities (no. 34). Therefore, instead of applying the tax to all inter-mediate use of output no. 5, we specify that it applies only to the intermediate use of no. 5 by no. 20. The petroleum tax in 1990 was $545.2 million (table 4-1), and the amount paid for crude oil by refineries was $117.8 billion (when the 1987 matrix is scaled to 1990); therefore the effective tax rate was 0.46 percent (column 3 of table 4-2). This effective tax rate matches very closely the statutory tax rate ($.097 a barrel) divided by the average price of oil in 1990 (about $20 a barrel).

Table 4-2. *Aggregation of SIC Industries into Forty-one Industry Categories, with Effective Tax Rates, 1990*

Our identification number	Standard industrial classification (SIC) numbers	Input tax rate (percent)[a]	EIT rate (percent)[b]	Description
1	01, 02	0	0.001	Agricultural products
2	07, 08, 09	0	0.002	Agricultural services, forestry, and fishing
3	10	0	0.025	Metal mining
4	11, 12	0	0.006	Coal mining
5	13	0.46	0.009	Crude petroleum and natural gas
6	14	0	0.008	Nonmetallic minerals (except fuels)
7	15, 16, 17	0	0.001	Construction
8	20	0	0.015	Food and kindred products
9	21	0	0.056	Tobacco manufacturers
10	22	0	0.006	Textile mill products
11	23	0	0.006	Apparel and other textile products
12	24	0	0.011	Lumber and wood products (except wood preserving)
13	2491	0	0.013	Wood preserving
14	25	0	0.006	Furniture and fixtures
15	26	0	0.021	Paper and allied products
16	27	0	0.012	Printing and publishing
17	28	0.31	0.099	Inorganic chemicals (2812, -16, -19, -73, -74, -79)
18	28	0.34	0.029	Organic chemicals (2813, -65, -69)
19	28	0	0.034	Chemicals and allied products (except preceding two items)
20	2911	0	0.151	Petroleum refining

		a	b	
21	29	0	0.105	Petroleum-related products
22	30	0	0.004	Rubber and miscellaneous plastic products
23	31	0	0.015	Leather and leather products
24	32	0	0.014	Stone, clay, and glass products
25	33	0	0.016	Primary metals industries
26	34	0	0.008	Fabricated metal products
27	35	0	0.018	Machinery, except electrical
28	36	0	0.023	Electrical and electronic equipment
29	37	0	0.025	Motor vehicles and transportation equipment
30	38	0	0.009	Instruments and related products
31	39	0	0.016	Miscellaneous manufacturing
32	40–47	0	0.007	Transportation
33	48	0	0.030	Communications
34	49	0	0.031	Electric, gas, and sanitary services
35	50–51	0	0.004	Wholesale trade
36	52–59	0	0.009	Retail trade
37	60–62,64,67	0	0.011	Finance
38	63	0	0.052	Insurance
39	65	0	0.001	Real estate
40	70–89	0	0.001	Services
41	91–97	0	0.000	Government enterprise and special industries

Sources: Author's calculations using data from "Benchmark Input-Output Accounts for the U.S. Economy, 1987," *Survey of Current Business*, vol. 74 (April 1994), pp. 73–115.

a. Effective rate of tax on intermediate input of each good, calculated for 1990 as tax liability over the sum of all its intermediate uses. For inputs not subject to the Superfund tax, the 1990 tax liability is zero.

b. Effective rate of the corporate environmental income tax (EIT) as a percent of value added in each industry, calculated for 1990 as EIT liabilities over value added.

The chemical feedstock taxes apply at different rates to various chemicals used by any industry. We aggregate all the industries producing taxed inorganic chemicals into one industry (no. 17), and then divide the observed tax in 1990 ($49.4 million, from table 4-1) by the total intermediate use of this output to find that the effective tax rate was 0.31 percent (column 3, table 4-2). Similarly, the observed tax on organic chemicals (no. 18) divided by the total intermediate use of this good yields an effective tax rate of 0.34 percent. For other inputs not subject to Superfund tax, we use effective rates of zero.

Many individual chemical products are known to be taxed at rates that approach 2 percent of their price.[34] Even with 480 industries, however, the input-output matrix does not separately identify these individual products. Some of the industries produce only untaxed chemicals (aggregated in our industry no. 19—chemicals and allied products), but most of the chemical industries in the list produce both taxed and untaxed chemicals. Thus our categories for inorganic chemicals (no. 17) and organic chemicals (no. 18) necessarily include some untaxed chemicals. In our model each industry produces one output, so this procedure effectively averages over the taxed and untaxed goods within an industry and applies that effective tax rate to the single output of the industry.

Column 4 of table 4-2 shows the effective rate of the corporate environmental income tax. The EIT actually applies to part of the profits for each firm, namely the modified alternative minimum taxable income that exceeds $2 million. More complicated general equilibrium models might be able to calculate the effect of this tax on the wage rate and the interest rate, and thus the extent to which the burden is passed backward onto labor and capital.[35] Our simpler model assumes fixed economywide rates of return to labor and capital, and therefore fixed value added in each industry. The effective tax rate for each industry is calculated as the EIT liability for that industry divided by value added in that industry. This rate then represents the percentage increase in value added that is required for each industry: labor and capital must produce enough to cover this tax as well as their returns. These higher costs are reflected in output prices and in the cost to other industries of buying those outputs as intermediate inputs. The ultimate burden is therefore passed on to consumers.

For each of the 41 industries, we have an equation that says the value of output (price times quantity) is equal to the cost of all the inputs (see appendix C). In long-run equilibrium, no firm receives excess profits. The cost side includes the price and amount of each intermediate input, and value added. The prices of three intermediate inputs are increased by the tax rates given in column 3 of table 4-2, and value added is increased by the tax rates in column 4. There are thus 41 equations that all involve the 41 prices and other variables. Because the equations are linear, we use matrix algebra to solve for the 41 prices as functions of the other variables (intermediate inputs, tax rates, and value added). In other words, we have a simultaneous solution for all prices, considering that each price depends on all other prices of goods that may be used as inputs. This procedure accounts not only for taxes on intermediate goods such as chemicals and petroleum, but also for the increased cost of some other intermediate inputs that may themselves be produced using chemicals or petroleum, or even other inputs that use chemicals or petroleum.

Assumptions

Several assumptions are necessary for our input-output model. To begin with, we assume that the demand for every industry's output is sufficiently large to accommodate plenty of firms, each of which achieves a size for which costs are minimized. In other words, entry barriers do not reduce the number of firms or the extent of competition. Because any change in output can be met by changes in the number of firms, all operating at minimum cost, the industry is competitive and marginal cost is constant. No firm makes abnormal profits in the long run after all prices and outputs have adjusted. To check the reasonableness of this assumption, we looked at the Commerce Department's four-firm concentration ratios that represent the percentage of each industry output produced by the largest four firms in the industry.[36] According to F. M. Scherer, when this ratio is less than 0.50, the industry is adequately competitive.[37] The ratios convince us that perfect competition and constant costs are adequate approximations of reality.

We also assume that input coefficients are fixed; thus each output must be produced using unchanged proportions of each intermediate input and value added. When one input price rises, producers cannot switch to using more of a different input. The model thus accounts for first-order effects on the price of an output that is produced using a mix of intermediate inputs, but not for second-order effects on changes in the mix. Also, therefore, our figures for tax revenue are only approximations. The model captures the effect on output price, so producers may decrease output by decreasing all inputs, but it misses the possibility that producers might switch from a taxed input to an untaxed input.

Assumptions must also be made about international trade. It cannot be assumed that the economy is perfectly open, with imports or exports of all goods, because then any attempted change in the price of the domestic good would induce purchasers to switch entirely to the foreign good. The price of each good in the United States would be completely determined by world markets and could not be affected by any domestic tax policy. We think Superfund taxes do affect prices. At the opposite extreme, it could be assumed that the economy is perfectly closed, with no imports or exports. In this case the domestic price for each good could be determined from information on the costs of production, as is done in our model. But this extreme is also too restrictive.

Fortunately, we do not have to assume a completely closed economy. Our model is valid under the less restrictive assumption that each domestic good is an imperfect substitute for the corresponding foreign good.[38] As long as the two goods are not identical, an increase in the price of the domestic good may induce purchasers to substitute incompletely toward the foreign good. This possibility makes demand for the domestic good more elastic (that is, makes the demand curve in figure 4-1 relatively flat). In other words, taxes are not good for international competitiveness because with taxes domestic production falls and imports rise. In figure 4-1, however, price is independent of the shape of the demand curve. The important point here is that the price of the domestic good is still determined by the location of the cost curve. The assumption of imperfect substitution is therefore consistent with our model because we merely assume that price is determined by the location of the cost curve.

Our model does not account for all possible indirect effects. For other purposes, one might want a general equilibrium model with multiple factors of production (such as labor and capital), multiple production sectors, and multiple consumer income groups, as well as demands for each final output. Such a model would account for changes in the wage rate for labor or the rate of return for capital. For our purposes, however, the simpler model provides meaningful and helpful results and avoids excessive complications. The model used here accounts for the most important effects of Superfund taxes on the prices of intermediate goods purchased by other industries, on the cost of producing those other outputs, and thus on the equilibrium prices of those other outputs.

Results for Existing Superfund Taxes

We begin by calculating prices in the absence of any Superfund taxes, then we insert each Superfund tax rate into the model and calculate new prices. We calculate the price increases separately for each of the three Superfund tax instruments—the petroleum tax, the chemical feedstocks tax, and the corporate environmental income tax. All results are expressed as the percentage increase in price, the price change divided by the old price.[39]

These effects on the prices of all 41 outputs are shown in figure 4-2. Effects of the petroleum tax are shown with gray bars. This tax is imposed on crude petroleum (no. 5) at a rate of 0.46 percent in 1990 (see table 4-2). Figure 4-2 shows that the price of crude petroleum hardly changes, but this net price must be multiplied by 1.0046 to get the gross-of-tax price paid by refineries that buy crude petroleum. Even then the tax rate is fairly small, as a hundred dollars of crude costs only an extra 46 cents. This tax raises the cost of production for refineries that buy crude oil, but the refineries also use other untaxed inputs. Thus the break-even price of refined petroleum (no. 20) rises only 0.30 percent. The higher price of refined petroleum then raises the cost of production of petroleum-related products (no. 21) and transportation (no. 32), but these two output prices rise by less than 0.1 percent.

The effects of chemical feedstock taxes are shown with white bars in figure 4-2. The price of inorganic chemicals (no. 17) rises by 0.06 percent and the price of organic chemicals (no. 18) by 0.08 percent. These output prices rise because some of the chemical firms purchase chemicals that are subject to tax. The firms' costs rise, so their output prices rise. If they sell taxed chemicals, their customers must pay the increased price plus the tax.[40] We therefore see slightly increased output prices for those who buy these taxed chemicals, including producers of textiles (no. 10), wood preserving products (no. 13), other chemicals (no. 19), and rubber and plastics (no. 22).

The black bars in figure 4-2 show the increases in price attributable to the environmental income tax. This tax burden is fairly diffuse, with no price rising by even 0.1 percent; the reason is that the tax applies to all industries rather than to specific intermediate inputs. Somewhat higher prices can be expected for industries that have high amounts of alternative minimum taxable income relative to value added, and for those that have high amounts of value added relative to other inputs. As it turns out, these industries are metal mining (no. 3), tobacco

Figure 4-2. *Price Increase for Outputs of Forty-one Industries under Each Current Superfund Tax*

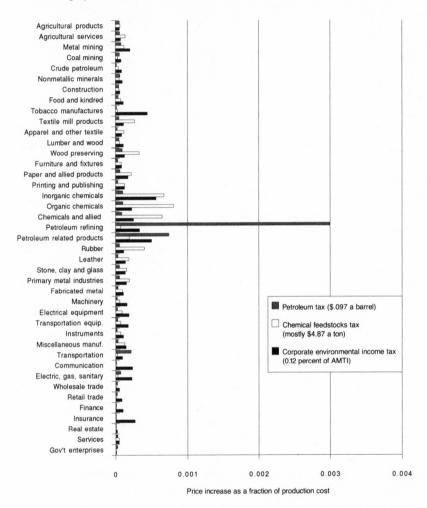

Source: Authors' calculations and appendix C. For the full name and number of each industry, see table 4-2.

manufactures (no. 9), chemicals (nos. 17, 18, 19), petroleum products (nos. 20, 21), and insurance (no. 38).

The three Superfund taxes added together are represented by the white bars in figure 4-3. It will be recalled from table 4-1 that the petroleum tax raised $545.2 million in 1990, chemical taxes raised

Figure 4-3. *Price Increase for Outputs of Forty-one Industries under Current Taxes and with an Extra $1 Billion in Petroleum Tax Revenue*

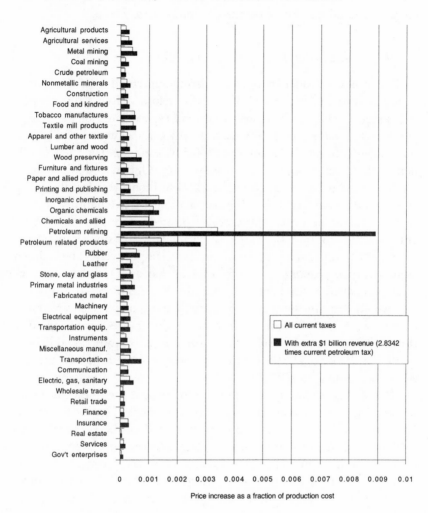

Price increase as a fraction of production cost

Source: See figure 4-2.

$286.2 million, and the EIT raised $520.2 million. Taxed crude oil is purchased by only one industry—petroleum refining (no. 20). Therefore this price rises the most, by 0.34 percent. Then the price of petroleum-related products (no. 21) rises by 0.14 percent. Because each of the three taxes separately was found to raise the price of various chemicals, all three taxes together raise the prices of these chemicals (by about 0.1 percent)—the second highest increase. Still the extra cost is only ten cents on a hundred dollars for these commodities.

Effects of Increasing Existing Superfund Taxes

We can now consider changes in existing Superfund taxes that might be required to finance some of the liability reforms discussed in chapter 3. As seen in chapter 2, annual trust fund expenditures for the current program (the status quo) have remained fairly constant at around $1.6 billion annually. In table 3-3, under option 1 we estimate that $585.0 million of that total would go to cleanup costs. Option 2 would require the trust fund to pay an additional $482.4 million a year for all cleanup at 220 co-disposal facilities. Elimination of retroactive liability at multiparty sites for hazardous substances deposited before 1980 (option 3), or before 1987 (option 4), would exceed annual status quo cleanup costs by $1,059.0 million or $1,395.0 million, respectively. The Clinton administration proposal to pay for orphan shares (option 5) would increase annual trust fund spending for site cleanups by $350.5 million, and would require another $367.5 million from taxes on insurance companies to pay for the environmental insurance resolution fund (EIRF). Thus the alternatives we examine could require an additional $350.5 million to $1,395.0 million a year in trust fund revenues for additional cleanup costs.

Each of these spending options could be matched with each different tax option, or even with multiple taxes, to raise the needed money. However, the many possible combinations need not be evaluated separately. For each tax option, we can calculate the effects on prices of raising $1 billion annually. This dollar amount is arbitrary, but effects are proportional: if the extra tax were to raise $2 billion, for example, effects on prices would be twice the amounts given here. First we calculate the effect on the prices for each of the forty-one industry outputs of raising an extra $1 billion annually from each of the three current Superfund taxes.

The black bars in figure 4-3 show the increases in the forty-one prices attributable to all current Superfund taxes plus an extra $1 billion in petroleum tax. To raise this tax from $545.2 million to $1,545.2 million, we must multiply the existing tax rate by 2.83. In other words, the effective rate rises from 0.46 percent to 1.30 percent (so the statutory rate must rise from 9.7 cents to 27.5 cents a barrel).[41] The price

Figure 4-4. *Price Increase for Outputs of Forty-one Industries under Current Taxes and with an Extra $1 Billion in Chemical Feedstocks Tax Revenue*

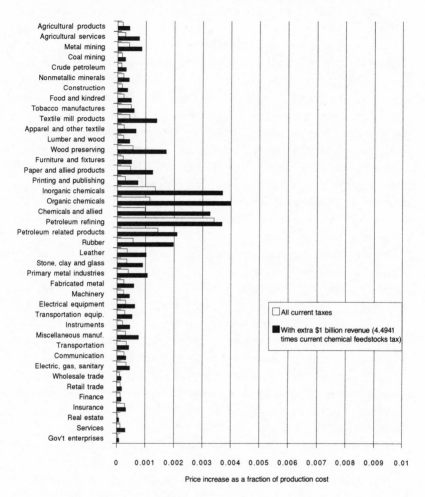

Price increase as a fraction of production cost

Source: See figure 4-2.

increase more than doubles for refined petroleum (no. 20). Other affected industries are users of refined petroleum such as petroleum-related products (no. 21) and transportation (no. 32).

The effects of increasing the chemical feedstock taxes are shown in figure 4-4. The white bars show the effects of existing Superfund taxes; the black bars represent all those taxes plus an extra $1 billion in the chemicals tax. The existing tax figure was $286.2 million, so the chemical feedstocks tax rates must all be raised by a factor of 4.49 to obtain $1,286.2 million. Thus the effective tax rate on inorganic chemicals rises from 0.31 to 1.39 percent, and that on organic chemicals rises from 0.34 to 1.53 percent. To achieve this change, actual tax rates would have to rise by the same proportion, that is, from $4.87 a ton to $21.87 a ton. As can be seen from figure 4-4, the price of organic chemicals would then rise by 0.4 percent.[42] The black bars are not proportional to the white bars because only chemical taxes are increased in this figure. In other words, the price increase for petroleum refining (no. 20) is largely unaffected by the additional chemical tax, and the (small) price increase more than doubles for textiles (no. 10), wood preserving (no. 13), and chemicals (nos. 17–19). Figure 4-4 shows nicely how the tax on just chemicals gets spread among virtually all of the forty-one industries. In every industry the black bar representing the tax with the added chemical tax is longer than the white bar representing existing taxes.

The effect of raising environmental income taxes from $520.2 million to $1,520.2 million is shown in figure 4-5. The effective tax rates (in column 4, table 4-2) would have to increase by a factor of 2.92, and the statutory rate would have to rise from 0.12 to 0.35 percent of AMTI above $2 million. The white bars represent existing taxes and the black bars represent price increases attributable to existing taxes plus the extra $1 billion EIT tax. The difference between black bars and white bars is the incremental effect of raising the EIT, which is largest for those industries most affected by EIT in the first place: metal mining (no. 3), tobacco manufactures (no. 9), chemicals (nos. 17, 18, 19), petroleum products (nos. 20, 21), and insurance (no. 38).

The implications of this analysis are that Superfund taxes are small and their effects diffuse. In CERCLA and SARA, Congress tried to target chemicals and petroleum, but the burden is felt in all industries through slightly higher costs of production. All price increases are substantially less than 1 percent.

Other Superfund Tax Proposals

Many different taxes have been proposed to finance Superfund cleanups of contaminated sites. The many issues associated with each are beyond the scope of this book. Nor do we discuss a proposal to use general revenues to supplement existing Superfund taxes, because such a dis-

Figure 4-5. *Price Increase for Outputs of Forty-one Industries under Current Taxes and with an Extra $1 Billion in Environmental Income Tax Revenue*

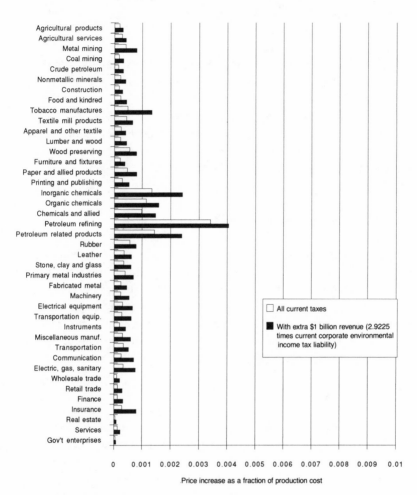

Source: See figure 4-2.

cussion would involve examining all economic effects of the federal tax system. Moreover, that proposal is unlikely to be implemented, given current efforts to cut the federal deficit. If, however, general revenues were to be used for Superfund without raising federal taxes, we would have to discuss the economic effects of an increased federal budget deficit and of cuts in other programs, which are also beyond the scope of this book.

Any new tax instrument would entail major one-time implementation costs as well as other fixed costs each year for administration by the Internal Revenue Service and compliance by taxpayers. It would not make sense to implement a major new tax and incur those large fixed costs for the amount of revenue required for Superfund. However, if the federal government were to implement a major new tax for some other reason (to replace an existing tax or for deficit reduction), it might be possible to raise the rate a bit to provide additional revenue to Superfund. One such tax would be a broad-based value added tax. A VAT has interested academic economists for years and is likely to be considered by Congress soon. If the federal deficit grows further, a value added tax might become not only possible but essential. Later we discuss the possibility of incrementing a value added tax and calculate effects of a VAT on prices.

Another proposal would impose a Superfund tax on premiums of commercial property-casualty insurance companies. The Clinton administration proposes such a tax to finance an environmental insurance resolution fund that would be used to facilitate the resolution of CERCLA claims by responsible parties against insurance companies. This proposal is described in detail in chapter 3, and the insurance industry is further analyzed in chapter 5; here we calculate the effect on prices of a tax on commercial property-casualty insurance. We also discuss in general some other proposals for Superfund taxes.

A Value Added Tax

Production of goods takes place in stages, often by different firms that buy various raw materials, transform them, and sell them to other firms. Each firm's value added is the value of what it sells minus the value of what it buys. This difference is the value contributed by the primary inputs, labor and capital. Therefore a value added tax would apply to a tax base defined as revenue from sales minus the cost of materials.[43] Moreover, the total value of a finished consumer good, such as an automobile, is just equal to the sum of the value added at each stage of production. Therefore if value added is taxed at all stages at a uniform rate, the result is conceptually equivalent to a sales tax on the finished product at the same rate.

For example, some mining firms buy machinery and sell coal for more than the cost of the machinery. The difference is value added. Other mining firms sell iron ore. Firms at the next stage buy coal and iron ore, add value, and sell steel. Still other firms buy steel and other inputs, add value, and sell products such as automobiles. Because the value of the automobiles matches the total value added at all stages of production, a value added tax at a 5 percent rate (on mining, steel, and automobile companies) would raise the same revenue as a 5 percent retail sales tax on automobiles alone.

This conceptual equivalence only holds if all activities are taxed at a uniform rate, which is not likely to occur. Any real-world value added tax could end up with exemptions for small firms, a graduated rate structure, no tax on financial service firms whose value added is hard to measure, and low or zero rates on products such as food and medicine that are viewed as necessities because they constitute a large proportion of low-income budgets. These exemptions and differential rates would distort consumer choices, reduce economic efficiency, and increase administrative and compliance costs, all in order to achieve greater equity by placing smaller burdens on low-income families.

Implementation of a value added tax would require major adjustment costs such as those entailed in hiring and training new auditors, designing and printing new tax forms, and explaining new provisions to taxpayers. The tax would require additional annual administration and compliance costs. It would have a broad base, however, and could collect large amounts of revenue at fairly low rates. The tax would not be worth implementing for the small amounts necessary for Superfund, but an existing value added tax could be incremented for Superfund.

The value added tax is sometimes described as a money machine because value added provides a large tax base. At a moderate 5 percent rate of tax, even a real-world VAT with many exemptions could collect more than $100 billion a year. We provide calculations here only for a perfectly uniform tax on all value added, rather than trying to guess which goods would receive exemptions. Using value added figures in our input-output model, we find that each percentage point would provide about $55 billion in revenue.[44] Thus an additional $1 billion for Superfund could be acquired with an incremental rate of only 0.018 percent.

The effects of a value added tax on prices in all forty-one industries are shown in figure 4-6. The effects of existing taxes are represented by white bars; the effects of adding the small $1 billion VAT represented by black bars. All industries experience a jump in their output prices, reflecting the jump in their costs. All prices rise by exactly 0.018 percent. All industries buy intermediate inputs that are 0.018 percent

Figure 4-6. *Price Increase for Outputs of Forty-one Industries under Current Taxes and with $1 Billion in Value Added Tax Revenue*

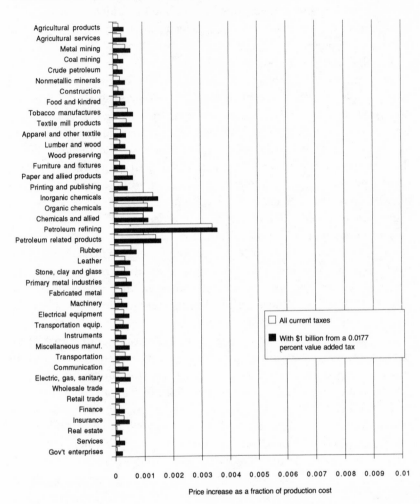

Source: See figure 4-2.

more expensive, and each pays a tax of 0.018 percent on their own value added, so all costs rise by 0.018 percent. This calculation confirms the assertion that a flat-rate value added tax is equivalent to a flat sales tax on all final outputs. Thus a VAT increment for Superfund would impose a most diffuse burden, a small increase in the price of all goods purchased by consumers.

A Tax on Property-Casualty Insurance

There is some doubt about whether the courts will find that commercial property-casualty insurance companies are liable under their commercial general liability policies for Superfund costs incurred by firms they insure or that they insured in the past. If reform of Superfund were to release from liability any of the firms that contributed waste to National Priorities List sites, not only would these firms benefit but their insurers would too. If a release of liability were to leave a revenue shortfall to be recovered through additional Superfund taxes, one view of equity might suggest a tax not only on those firms but also on insurers.

In the Clinton administration proposal, an environmental insurance resolution fund would help avoid litigation over insurance coverage by providing money to firms that settle. Under the current version, revenues for the EIRF would come from a retrospective tax of 0.20 to 0.27 percent on part of commercial insurance premiums collected between January 1, 1971, and December 31, 1985 (expected to raise $2.17 billion over five years) and from a prospective tax of 0.34 to 0.44 percent on new premiums (expected to raise $930 million over five years). Only the prospective tax might be expected to influence directly the cost of buying new commercial insurance. These rates and revenues would probably be modified by Congress before enactment of the proposal. To continue to compare results across all Superfund tax proposals, we use the input-output model to calculate the effects of raising $1 billion a year from a property-casualty insurance tax. Effects are proportional, so a prospective tax on insurance that would raise $1 billion over five years would have one-fifth of the effect given by our calculations.

The input-output model has only one industry and one output for insurance carriers (no. 38), and about half is commercial property-casualty insurance.[45] In the model we cannot distinguish a tax on property-casualty insurers from a tax on other insurers, but in the model an extra $1 billion a year could be raised by a tax of 2.05 percent on all intermediate uses of the output of insurance. We have no estimates of elasticities with which to predict a decline in demand for insurance. It should be noted, however, that the proposed tax might encourage nontrivial self-insurance.

A new tax on property-casualty insurance clearly would affect the insurance industry in the short run as insurance companies scaled back

Figure 4-7. *Price Increase for Outputs of Forty-one Industries under Current Taxes and with $1 Billion of Tax on Commercial Property and Casualty Insurance*

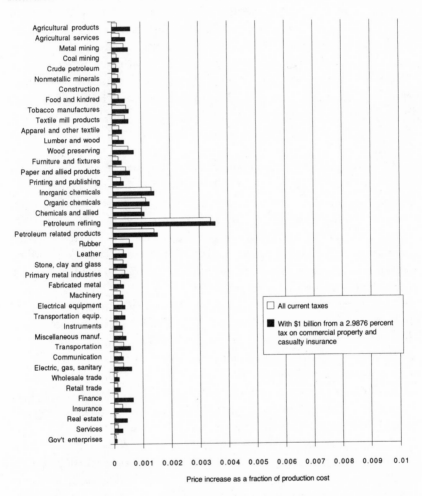

Price increase as a fraction of production cost

Source: See figure 4-2.

or otherwise adjusted to the imposition of the tax (see chapter 5). Our use of the input-output model shows the effects on prices in the new long-run equilibrium after all adjustments. These effects are illustrated in figure 4-7. The results are striking. Other firms pay the 2.05 percent tax on their purchase of insurance, but the net price received by insurance companies hardly changes. Instead, costs rise for all the firms that purchase insurance. And because every firm buys at least some insurance, every output price must rise a little to cover that cost. Figure 4-7 shows that output prices for all forty-one industries rise only slightly. The incidence of this tax is almost as widely spread as that of the value added tax.

A property-casualty insurance tax, like any new tax, would impose administrative and compliance costs for both implementation and annual collections. Faced with the tax and higher costs, firms might buy less insurance. Nothing is wrong with buying insurance, so the disincentive of the tax might create excess burden. Insurance is not a polluting product that ought to be discouraged for reasons of economic efficiency. Rather, the justification for the property-casualty tax proposal is based solely on the perceived equity of taxing firms that would benefit from a liability release. Yet all firms would face higher costs and thus would charge higher prices to consumers. Again, Congress might impose some short-run costs on insurance companies, but it cannot legislate the long-run burden of the tax.

Some Superfund reform proposals include an unspecified tax on small businesses, partly to balance the existing environmental income tax on large businesses (those with more than $2 million in alternative minimum taxable income). It is not clear what would be gained by such a tax. The original Superfund taxes on chemicals and petroleum were intended to target specific industries, though our input-output analyses showed that the effects of these taxes were diffuse. The EIT was intended to spread its burden widely. An unspecified tax on small businesses would introduce yet another set of tax forms, as would the separate tax on insurance companies. Thus under these proposals the Superfund program would depend on at least five taxes, each with its own administrative structure and compliance costs, in order to spread widely the burden of collecting a mere $2 billion or $3 billion a year. The same total Superfund revenue, with the same widespread burdens, could be achieved with no separate administrative structure simply by raising all regular personal and corporate income tax rates about one-tenth of 1 percent.

Other Proposals

Other additional taxes have been suggested to finance Superfund, such as a national sales tax or a corporate receipts tax. A national sales tax would have effects identical to those of a value added tax. A corporate receipts tax would apply to a broad definition of corporate income, with deductions only for the cost of goods sold. This tax cannot be analyzed appropriately in our input-output model, so we cannot estimate price effects. We know, however, that price effects would be diffuse because the tax would be collected from all industries. Either the sales tax or the corporate receipts tax proposals would involve introducing a major new U.S. tax system, with its costs of implementation, auditing, enforcement, and compliance by taxpayers (who would have to learn a new set of tax rules). These costs are not worth incurring for the small amount of revenue required for Superfund. If introduced for some other reason, however, such a tax could be increased slightly for Superfund.

Still another proposal would raise the environmental income tax by reducing the $2 million threshold and taxing more of firms' alternative minimum taxable income. The price effects of this proposal cannot be calculated because we do not have specific information on the AMTI of individual firms; we have only the EIT paid in each industry and the value added in each industry. In discussing compliance cost, however, we showed that newly taxed firms could easily spend more on accountants than on tax payments.

Some have suggested a federal tipping fee on all solid waste disposal, or a waste-end tax on hazardous wastes alone. Tipping fees should probably be left to state and local governments, and a waste-end tax might be difficult to implement and enforce. No current data provide the number of hazardous waste generators or the amount of each type of waste generated.[46] There would be easy opportunities to avoid a waste-end tax: firms might use cheap on-site disposal methods that would be hard to capture within the purview of the tax, or illegal methods such as midnight dumping to evade the tax. Still, a waste-end tax is supposed to induce firms to reduce disposal amounts—and to make consumers pay for the full environmental costs of the goods they buy.

A waste-end tax has already been tried by the federal government. The Comprehensive Environmental Response, Compensation, and Liability Act of 1980 not only established the Hazardous Substance Response Trust Fund (Superfund) to deal with abandoned contaminated sites, but also established the Post-Closure Liability Trust Fund (PCLTF) to ensure continued long-term monitoring and care at other closed hazardous waste disposal facilities.[47] The PCLTF was financed by a tax on hazardous waste that would remain at qualified disposal facilities, at a rate of $2.13 a dry-weight ton. This tax would not be imposed during any year in which the balance in the fund exceeded $200 million.

The Post-Closure Liability Trust Fund and waste-end tax had a long list of problems. To begin with, the legislation did not define a dry-weight ton. Presumably the intent was to exclude the water component of different wastes to make them comparable, but the result was administrative complexity. Also the tax base excluded the overwhelming majority of waste—waste not sent to qualified facilities but managed on site.[48] Moreover, the tax and the fund applied to land-disposal facilities such as a landfills and surface impoundments; to the extent that the fund helped insure firms undertaking land disposal, it conflicted with the stated goal of the Hazardous and Solid Waste Amendments of 1984 to minimize the disposal of hazardous wastes in the land. Finally, the $200 million limit was not enough to cover likely liability claims. The Environmental Protection Agency estimated that the fund would have less than a 10 percent chance of remaining in positive balance after one hundred years.[49]

Faced with a revenue shortfall that contradicted a national policy to discourage land disposal of hazardous waste, Congress in the Superfund Amendments and Reauthorization Act of 1986 repealed the PCLTF and refunded all amounts that had been collected.[50] Congress is unlikely to reverse course a second time and reintroduce a waste-end tax for Superfund.

Summary and Implications

This chapter has evaluated Superfund taxes with respect to several criteria, including administrative and compliance costs, economic efficiency, concepts of equity, and effects on output prices. All these analyses point toward the conclusion that taxes designed specifically for Superfund do not operate as intended and have some unfortunate consequences.

First, they impose high administrative and compliance costs compared to the small amounts of revenue collected. Each separate tax entails an initial cost of implementation plus annual fixed costs of administration for the Internal Revenue Service and for compliance by taxpayers. These fixed costs are related to the forms needed to calculate the tax base and therefore fall as a percentage of revenue as the tax rate is increased. Superfund imposes many separate calculations and then imposes very low rates, such as 9.7 cents a barrel for petroleum or 22 cents a ton for a particular chemical. The worst offender is probably the environmental income tax, which requires complicated calculations of alternative minimum taxable income in excess of $2 million and then imposes a tax rate of only 0.12 percent. The compliance cost of this tax could range between 100 percent and 400 percent of the revenue collected. Thus Superfund taxes are no more—and might be even less—efficient than the liability scheme in raising revenues. Virtually all of the costs could be saved by using one simple tax, especially a preexisting tax, and then raising its rate to collect enough revenue for Superfund.

Second, in regard to economic efficiency, Superfund taxes might be thought to result in a small excess burden because the rates are so low, but such a conclusion would ignore preexisting taxes and other distortions. On the one hand, if existing taxes on petroleum already reduce the quantity of oil below the socially efficient level, an additional 9.7 cents in Superfund tax could have a disproportionately high welfare cost for consumers. On the other hand, if the consumption of oil is already greater than the socially efficient level because of sulfur dioxide emissions or global warming, an additional 9.7 cents in Superfund tax could increase social welfare. Thus we cannot say whether excess burden is positive or negative.

Third, existing Superfund taxes are not really in the spirit of either the polluter pays principle or the beneficiary pays principle. The petroleum and chemical taxes were set originally by looking at the nature of hazardous substances at existing Superfund sites, but their burdens are unlikely to fall either on the original managers or stockholders of the firms that were responsible for the pollution or on the past consumers who benefited from low prices that did not cover the environmental costs of production. Instead, these Superfund taxes raise the cost of producing new outputs and are therefore likely to be passed forward through higher prices to new consumers.

And fourth, Congress cannot target specific burdens in the long run. Any taxed industry may bear the costs of adjustment in the short run, but its output price is likely to increase to cover the new cost of production in the long run. When that output is used as an input to production in other industries, all prices must rise. The ultimate burdens are diffuse, rather than targeted, as revealed in our calculations using the input-output model. Together these results imply that Superfund taxes impose high compliance costs by trying unsuccessfully to target certain industries that cannot be targeted anyway.

CHAPTER FIVE

Superfund and the Insurance Industry

T HE SUPERFUND statute does not mention or identify the insurance industry as a source of funds for site cleanups. Property-casualty insurers, however, have been brought into the Superfund financing system by their insureds, the responsible parties, who claim that their own legal and cleanup costs are covered by commercial general liability policies they bought from property-casualty insurers.[1] Because of the often very high economic stakes involved, so-called coverage disputes between responsible parties and insurers are now found in courts throughout the country.

We begin this chapter by outlining the role of liability insurance in the debate over Superfund financing, then examine the nature and extent of Superfund's financial impact on the insurance industry under current law. We next explore the effects of possible changes in the liability system on insurers, assuming that revenues lost from the liability changes would be made up, at least in part, by revenues collected from a tax on insurance premiums. We also discuss the impact of possible taxes or assessments on insurance premiums designed to replace at least some of the current liability-based financing.

The Role of the Insurance Industry

For the commercial property-casualty insurance industry there are two major categories of Superfund-related expenses: those incurred in the process of apportioning liability for site cleanups, referred to as transaction costs, and those for payment of liability for actual cleanups, that is, indemnity payments. Insurers have thus far paid far more for the former than for the latter.

Specifically, some insurers have advanced funds under the duty-to-defend clauses of their policies to reimburse responsible parties for the parties' legal expenses in their disputes with the Environmental Protection Agency, state or local governments, and other responsible parties over the allocation of cleanup costs. Insurers who have done so, however, have also reserved the right to seek recovery of those advances if courts entitle them to do so.[2] But insurers argue that they are not liable in any way for actual cleanup expenses or costs of remediation incurred by the responsible parties they insured. Thus at the same time that insurers are reimbursing their insured responsible parties for defense costs, they also are incurring their own legal costs as a result of coverage disputes.

Although insurers have raised several other coverage defenses when disputing their liability, they have most often cited the standard pollution exclusion clause used in commercial general liability policies in effect from 1970 through 1985 to argue that the insurance did not apply. That exclusion states that it applies "to bodily injury or property *damage* arising out of the discharge, dispersal, release or escape of smoke, vapors, soot, fumes, acids, alkalis, toxic chemicals, liquids or gases, waste materials or other irritants, contaminants or pollutants into or upon land, the atmosphere, or any water course or body of water; but this exclusion does not apply if such discharge, dispersal, release or escape is *sudden and accidental* [emphasis added]."[3] Insurers have essentially argued that this language excludes coverage for cleanup expenses, which they claim are caused not by "sudden and accidental" pollution such as an explosion, but instead by the routine and gradual discharge of hazardous substances. Insurers have also argued that the costs associated with government-mandated cleanups are not damages within the meaning of the standard policy, but instead are merely injunctive or equitable obligations imposed on the policyholder by the government.

Responsible parties have disputed the insurers on both grounds. They have argued that the "sudden and accidental" requirement means that coverage remains for cleanup of hazardous substances whose release was neither "expected" nor "intended." Responsible parties have also asserted that cleanup costs are precisely the kind of damages for which commercial general liability policies were designed to compensate them.

So far, the courts appear to be about evenly divided on the meaning of the "sudden and accidental" language, although they almost uniformly side with the responsible parties on the damages question.[4] Still, insurers have so far paid little for remediation, because relatively few coverage disputes have been finally decided. Moreover, even in those cases in which responsible parties have prevailed on the issue of how the pre-1986 contract language should be interpreted, they must persuade juries that releases of substances were unintended or unexpected and convince judges that they have met other relevant legal tests (such as those involving choice of law, jurisdiction, or venue).

In 1986 insurers revised the standard pollution exclusion in their policies to eliminate essentially *all* coverage for pollution, including "sudden and accidental" releases. Insurers have had little difficulty in persuading courts to accept their interpretation of the newer language. Nevertheless, because some courts have not yet provided definitive guidance as to the meaning of the pre-1986 exclusion language, much uncertainty has remained over who should bear the cost of cleaning up sites where hazardous substances were deposited before 1986, when the newer clearer language was introduced. This is because interpretations of insurance contracts are generally matters of state law and thus do not present the kind of question that the federal courts can resolve. As a result, there are and will continue to be different ways of interpreting the commercial general liability exclusion in different states; some decisions will favor the insurer, others the insured. And even though state courts may gradually clarify the meaning of the exclusion language, trial courts still will be required to decide the many factual issues that are specific to each site.

Notwithstanding these difficulties, in early 1994 a group of responsible parties and insurers, calling itself the Coalition on Superfund, worked with the Clinton administration and congressional staff to develop a plan that would resolve much of the uncertainty surrounding disputes between insurers and responsible parties over Superfund liability. Under the proposed plan, which is embodied in H.R. 3800 (as discussed in chapter 3), an environmental insurance resolution fund (EIRF, discussed in chapter 3) would be established to cover the cost of cleanup of contamination that took place before 1986. Insurance companies would finance the EIRF through fees of $8.1 billion over a ten-year period. Responsible parties would apply to the EIRF, rather than to their individual insurers, for reimbursement of cleanup costs.

To protect insurers against having to pay $8.1 billion in taxes to finance the EIRF while still being subject to litigation by responsible parties over insurance coverage, the legislation would require that 85 percent of the responsible parties in litigation with their insurers on January 1, 1994, agree to accept payment from the EIRF and discontinue litigation.[5] If this "referendum" is not successful, the EIRF would be disbanded. Even if 85 percent of responsible parties endorse the EIRF and the referendum passes, responsible parties could still decline the EIRF's reimbursement offer and pursue recovery through litigation. But if they won less in court than the EIRF would have paid them, they would have to pay 50 percent of the insurers' court costs. This provision is intended to discourage responsible parties from litigating and to encourage them to seek compensation from the environmental insurance resolution fund, thus reducing transaction costs.

A key aspect of the coalition's proposal is that compliance is not strictly voluntary, but it would require legislative enactment. The proposal became part of the Clinton administration bill (H.R. 3800), described in chapter 3, and has garnered considerable support as a means of reducing transaction costs without gutting Superfund's liability scheme.

Whether private or government-mandated, any contribution by insurers to cleanup funds can be viewed as a tax on insurance premiums and modeled as such, as we have done in chapter 4.

Insurers' Financial Exposure under Superfund

How would insurers ultimately be affected by cleanup of National Priorities List sites under current law? This matter is complicated. First, the eventual scope of the cleanup effort is not known. For this reason we present estimates of the cost to insurers based on two scenarios of cleanup activity. One is grounded on our estimates of the total cost of cleaning up current National Priorities List sites, as presented in chapter 3, where cleanup of these sites is projected to be complete by 2003. A second scenario is grounded on a base case estimate, developed by the Congressional Budget Office, of the cost of cleaning up all current and future nonfederal NPL sites; this estimate extends to 2073.[6]

Another complication is that it is difficult, if not impossible, to predict court decisions regarding the interpretation and applicability of the commercial general liability exclusion for cleanup expenses. Depending on how these cases are decided, insurers could face quite small—or potentially huge—indemnity payments.

Third, determining how insurers would be affected is difficult because there are not one but two insurance industries that stand to be affected by future court decisions on coverage. Our principal focus is on the exposure of the primary (so-called direct excess) insurance carriers to claims filed by responsible parties. These insurers theoretically are first in line to bear any costs that otherwise might be borne by responsible parties. However, it is likely that many primary insurers would file claims with their reinsurers, pointing to clauses in their agreements that require reinsurers to "follow the fortunes" of the primary insurers. To date, reinsurers have paid little under these provisions because primary insurers have shouldered little direct liability. If the primary carriers eventually do file claims with their reinsurers, the reinsurance industry may not bear a significant share of the overall financial burden, for reasons discussed later.

Fourth, there also remains considerable uncertainty about the insurers' exposure to claims for legal costs, or transaction costs, under duty-to-defend clauses, although this uncertainty may be considerably less than that for actual cleanup costs. For example, the RAND Institute for Civil Justice has estimated that transaction costs incurred by responsible parties have so far averaged 21 percent of their total outlays.[7] How much of this total eventually will be borne by insurers is unknown. Nevertheless, insurers will continue to incur transaction costs for contesting efforts by responsible parties to hold them liable for cleanup costs (that is, for coverage disputes.)

Indeed, the RAND survey suggests that so far insurers have spent more on coverage disputes than on reimbursement of responsible parties' cleanup expenses. This should not be surprising, because insurers so far have spent very little on cleanup. Of their total outlays, just 12 percent have been for cleanup costs, that is, for indemnity payments. An estimated 42 percent have been on legal fees for coverage disputes; 37 percent have been for reimbursing the transaction costs of responsible parties under duty-to-defend provisions. The remaining 9 percent of insurers' outlays have gone to internal claims investigations.[8] Lloyd Dixon of RAND has estimated that once cleanup of National Priorities List sites is complete, indemnity payments will rise to 31 percent of insurers' expenditures, with 33 percent of all expenditures going to coverage disputes and 29 percent to covering duty-to-defend costs. An estimated 7 percent would go to internal claims investigations.[9]

In 1994, A. M. Best, one of the nations' leading rating agencies for insurers, estimated that the insurance industry has yet to recognize between $45 billion and $593 billion in undiscounted costs required

Table 5-1. *Estimated Financial Impact of Superfund Cleanup Liabilities on U.S. Insurers, under Three Cost Levels*
Billions of dollars unless otherwise specified

Cost category	Costs for current NPL sites			Costs for current and future NPL sites		
	Low	Medium	High	Low	Medium	High
1. Gross cleanup costs, undiscounted	33	33	33	228	228	228
2. Less trust fund contributions and amount paid by self-insured responsible parties (assumed to be 40 percent of gross costs)	−13	−13	−13	−91	−91	−91
3. Potential claims on insurers (row 1 minus row 2)	20	20	20	137	137	137
4. Assumed percentage of cleanup costs paid by insurers	30	40	50	30	40	50
5. Cleanup costs paid by insurers (row 3 times row 4)	6	8	10	41	55	69
6. Assumed share of transaction costs paid by insurers (as a percentage of gross cleanup costs, row 1)	15	20	25	15	20	25
7. Transaction costs paid by insurers (row 6 times row 1)	5	7	8	34	46	57
8. Total paid by insurers, undiscounted (row 5 plus row 7)	11	15	18	75	101	126

Source: Authors' estimates and, for gross cleanup costs for current and future National Priorities List sites, the base case developed in Congressional Budget Office, *The Total Costs of Cleaning Up Nonfederal Superfund Sites* (1994), p. 16.

for Superfund cleanups over the next twenty-five years.[10] (The corresponding discounted range of reserve additions would be $29 billion to $232 billion.) Unrecognized liabilities for sites on the National Priorities List make up the bulk of these costs. A. M. Best estimated that reserves needed for NPL sites alone would range from $23 billion to $475 billion. The remaining unrecognized liabilities are for sites not on the list; in other words, cleanups at these sites would be conducted under state Superfund laws or voluntarily by responsible parties. These are typically referred to as non-NPL sites.

In developing estimates of possible insurance industry exposure to Superfund expenses, we use a methodology similar to that pioneered by Amy Bouska, a principal with Tillinghast A. Towers Perrin Company, and subsequently refined by A. M. Best.[11] Our projections, shown in table 5-1, are based on two scenarios: our estimate of $33 billion for the total cost of cleaning up the 1,134 nonfederal sites currently on the National Priorities List (presented in chapter 3), and the Congressional

Budget Office (CBO) base case of $228 billion in gross costs for cleaning up 4,500 current and future nonfederal NPL sites in the next seventy to eighty years (this cost would be about $74 billion when discounted at an annual rate of 7 percent).[12]

In our estimates, we focus on undiscounted costs (row 1 in table 5-1) because current regulatory accounting rules generally do not permit insurers to discount their future losses for purposes of establishing loss reserves. It should be noted that undiscounted costs ignore that the current burden of responsible parties' making claims in the future is less than the cost of meeting these obligations today. And as Milton Russell, E. William Colglazier, and Mary English have observed, the highly uncertain timing of cleanup expenditures makes it difficult to discount them.[13] Nevertheless, we recognize that for other purposes, such as measuring the ability of the economy as a whole to bear cleanup costs, even rough discounted cost estimates might be more useful.[14]

We deduct from gross cleanup costs the costs of various items for which insurers are not likely to be responsible (row 2 in table 5-1). These include the costs of orphan shares (costs not picked up by responsible parties or their insurers), costs paid by self-insured responsible parties (generally larger companies that do not carry commercial general liability policies), and costs picked up by federal agencies (where they are responsible parties at nonfederal sites).[15] We assume that these deductions would average 40 percent of gross cleanup costs.

We then postulate that insurers would bear from 30 percent to 50 percent of the remaining totals, depending on how successful the insurers proved to be in their coverage litigation with responsible parties (row 4, table 5-1). This range is in line with the environmental insurance resolution fund provision in H.R. 3800, which sets reimbursement rates of 20, 40, or 60 percent, depending on the state venue. We collapse this range somewhat, because the average over all states is likely to be a narrower range. Taking our cost-sharing assumptions into account, we find that insurers may be required to pay from $6 billion to $10 billion in (undiscounted) cleanup costs for current National Priorities List sites and $41 billion to $69 billion in (undiscounted) cleanup costs for current and future NPL sites (row 5, table 5-1).

Insurers may, and almost certainly will, continue to bear some responsibility for their insureds' legal costs under the duty-to-defend provisions of commercial general liability policies. Insurers are also certain to continue spending money for their own legal fees, for their coverage disputes with responsible parties, and potentially with reinsurers. In our low-cost scenarios we assume that these transaction costs will equal 15 percent of total cleanup costs (row 6, table 5-1).[16] Our medium- and high-cost scenarios assume that transaction costs borne by insurers increase to 20 and 25 percent of cleanup costs, respectively. The scenarios also assume that insurers are less successful in recovering their advances to responsible parties and that although certain legal issues relating to responsible party liability and coverage may be clarified, the steady expansion of the number of responsible parties caught in Superfund's liability net would add transaction costs that more than compensate for any clarification of certain legal questions by the courts.

A key result in our estimates can be shown by comparing estimated insurer transaction costs (row 7) with estimated insurer cleanup costs (row 5). In the low-cost scenarios, insurers' exposure to transaction costs is slightly less than their exposure to cleanup costs. In the mid-cost scenarios, however, insurers' exposure to transaction costs accounts for about 45 percent of total financial exposure. These results are especially important. Unlike projections of cleanup costs, which are highly uncertain and depend on the outcome of numerous judicial decisions and possibly settlement negotiations, it is far more likely that insurers will continue to bear significant transaction costs.

Estimates of the total Superfund-related costs that insurers are likely to bear range from a low of $11 billion for the current National Priorities List sites to a high of $126 billion over about eighty years for current and future NPL sites (an annual figure of $1.6 billion). The annual cost in the high-cost scenario for current and future sites is 24 percent less than the $2.1 billion projected annually for the next ten years to complete cleanup of current NPL sites alone. However, in the high-cost case the annual costs continue to be incurred for eight decades and for four times the number of sites currently on the National Priorities List.

The estimates in table 5-1 are based on an assumption that primary insurers would bear all the cleanup costs borne by the insurance industry and would not receive reimbursement from reinsurers. To the extent that this is not the case, the financial impact on the primary insurance industry would be less severe, although the net impact on consumers of insurance could conceivably be worse (a possibility discussed later).

Our high estimates are lower than the high estimates of A. M. Best, primarily because both we and the Congressional Budget Office are less pessimistic about overall cleanup costs. We also make allowance (in our low-cost case in particular) for the possibility that insurers will prevail in one way or another in most of the coverage disputes in which they may be involved. A. M. Best is less optimistic (from the insurers' point of view) in this regard as well.

Consequences of Insurer Liability

The projected Superfund-related costs that the insurance industry could be required to bear cannot be well understood unless they are compared with the financial resources of the industry, and more precisely with the resources of the individual companies that would be responsible. Unfortunately, from publicly available information it is impossible to determine the exposure of individual insurers to cleanup expenses (or to other extraordinarily large risks). Thus we are compelled to concentrate solely on the consequences at the industry level and for consumers of insurance, both commercial and personal.

At first blush it may appear that the cost burdens implied under the scenarios shown in table 5-1, although sizable, would not materially affect the insurance industry because insurers could be expected to pass the costs on to consumers. For example, in 1991 underwriters of "other liability and product liability" insurance, an insurance category that is mostly coincident with commercial general liability coverage, collected almost $17 billion in premium revenue.[17] If these insurers were required to bear additional Superfund-related costs of as much as $1.6 billion annually—the cost projection in our high-cost scenario for current and future National Priorities List sites—they would have to raise their premiums 9 percent to cover the cost. This would be a stiff increase, to be sure, but one that does not appear unduly alarming.

It is highly doubtful, however, that insurers would be able to implement such a premium increase. That insurers have vigorously contested their liability for cleanup expenses suggests that at the time they wrote the commercial general liability policies in question they neither expected to pay claims of such magnitude nor fully built those expectations into their premiums. Accordingly, any expenses they may be required to bear in the future for cleanup, as well as any legal costs, are akin to sunk costs. In a competitive market (subject to one qualification) insurers would not be able to pass on to their current commercial liability customers the higher costs associated with past hazardous waste cleanup claims. In other words, new insurers, unencumbered by a legacy of past liabilities, could underprice any firms seeking to pass on old liabilities.

The qualification to this is that the sunk costs arising from the older policies could suddenly become current costs of doing business for all insurers in the event that Superfund-related expenses trigger insurer insolvencies. In all fifty states, property-casualty insurers finance guaranty funds that honor the claims of policyholders of insurers that fail (generally up to $300,000). In the event of failure, the funds assess all insurers doing business in the state for the cost of providing this protection up to a ceiling amount for each year (in most states the ceiling is no higher than 2 percent of new premiums). If the claims costs exceed that level, the assessments continue at the ceiling level until all policyholders are paid off. Accordingly, if Superfund-related expenses were to cause some insurers to fail, property-casualty insurers (current and new) generally would be exposed to potentially higher guaranty fund assessments, and thus higher costs for all new policies, of up to 2 percent for a finite period of years, until claims costs were paid off.

Recent experience suggests that for this to happen to any significant extent the claims and other costs that insurers must pay would have to be substantially higher than the $18 billion liability projected in our high-cost scenario for current National Priorities List sites alone. The $15.5 billion in claims costs resulting from Hurricane Andrew—the most costly single event in the history of the insurance industry—caused a surprisingly small number of insolvencies.[18] Fewer than a dozen small, Florida-based insurers out of hundreds doing business in the state actually failed in the wake of the hurricane, triggering what are likely to be relatively modest guaranty fund assessments. However, even our low-cost scenario for current and future NPL sites—$75 billion—would be a shock to insurers, with claims more than four times the size of those for Hurricane Andrew.

It is tempting to argue that some commercial insurers could have sufficient power in certain segments of the market to pass on some of the costs related to old policies and thus not absorb all the losses in the industry's surplus. This is unlikely because the commercial insurance industry is not highly concentrated; thus no single insurer is likely to have sufficient market power to bring this result about. In 1991 the largest underwriter of general liability insurance, American International Group (AIG), had less than 20 percent of the market, and the top eight such underwriters collectively had 46 percent, a concentration level not indicative of a market in which suppliers have significant market power.[19]

In short, it is likely that insurers—or more precisely, their shareholders (including policyholders of mutual companies)—will bear most if not all of any claims and legal costs they may be required to pay in connection with Superfund cleanups. It is nevertheless tempting to dismiss the size of the impact of these costs. After all, the property-casualty insurance industry at year-end 1993 had about $180 billion in capital and in recent years has been earning more than $12 billion annually. Thus even a negative cost of as much as $1.6 billion—the annual cost in our high-cost scenario—seemingly would only slow the rate of increase in the industry's capital.

But such a view ignores the potentially substantial short-run disruption to insurance markets, and insurance consumers, that could result if state insurance regulators, federal securities regulators, or the insurers' accountants begin to require the industry to establish much larger reserves for Superfund costs. In that event the additional reserves for hazardous waste cleanups would immediately reduce insurers' surplus or capital by far greater amounts than would the annual payments of cleanup claims and legal costs. If sufficiently substantial, a reduction in capital could restrict the premium-writing capacity of the affected insurers, forcing them to raise more capital, cut back insurance availability, and increase premium rates.[20]

So far we have been able to identify only a few insurers who have set up reserves specifically related to Superfund expenses; the amounts they have reserved are modest.[21] In conversations with industry experts we have also learned that other insurers have recognized the likelihood of future transaction costs by adding to their general reserves for "loss adjustment expenses." In these cases, Superfund-specific transaction costs cannot be identified from publicly available data, although the general reserve account may be larger because of expected Superfund-related transaction costs. Nevertheless, there is no evidence that commercial insurers have yet added reserve amounts to their loss adjustment expenses on the order of the estimated transaction costs in table 5-1. The required reserves for these transaction costs alone could be extremely large: $46 billion in our medium scenario for current and future National Priorities List sites (an amount exceeding the total insured cost of Hurricane Andrew), and roughly $57 billion in our high-cost scenario for current and future NPL sites.

The events following Hurricane Andrew provide some indication of how insurance consumers can be hurt by a major loss of surplus that, on the surface, appeared to affect only the insurance companies themselves, and that resulted in a surprisingly small number of insurer insolvencies. Shortly after the hurricane, some of the largest insurers doing business in Florida threatened either to leave the state or significantly to curtail the amount of coverage they would provide in the state. The Florida legislature responded by imposing a moratorium on policy cancellations through the end of the 1993 hurricane season. Nevertheless, many of Florida's largest insurers of homeowners have refused to write new policies and have raised premiums on all current policies.[22]

If anything, Florida's experience with Hurricane Andrew understates what could happen to insurance markets if insurers were required to bear substantial Superfund-related costs. It is one thing for events such as Hurricane Andrew to cause insurers to rethink their willingness to continue serving markets that suddenly seem to pose uninsurable risks, or to charge substantially more for insuring such risks. It is another matter for insurers to suffer such significant shocks to surplus that their ability to underwrite risks they want to underwrite is impaired.

In the abstract, it is virtually impossible to estimate how much coverage would actually be curtailed and for how long without knowing the size of any additional reserves for Superfund-related expenses that regulators might require of specific insurers. In the absence of such information, it cannot be determined which insurers might confront a deficiency in capital. Moreover, it is conceivable, if not likely, that certain larger publicly held insurers would be able to replace some portion of any loss in surplus by issuing new stock. As a result, for any given loss in surplus the largest cutbacks in insurance availability would be made by the smaller insurers and those that are mutually owned by their policyholders and thus unable to access the capital markets.

Nevertheless, it is sobering to compare the industry's liability for Superfund-related costs with the capital of the largest underwriters of commercial liability insurance. According to A. M. Best, the nation's forty-seven largest commercial liability underwriting organizations (excluding large, predominantly personal-line insurers that have limited environmental exposures) had $65 billion in total capital at year-end 1992. Thus if insurers were required to establish reserves of $75 billion for our estimated low-cost scenario for current and future NPL sites (table 5-1), the surplus of the property-casualty insurance industry would be completely eliminated. The $126 billion for the high-cost scenario would wipe out the industry almost twice over. Only if the insurers faced costs in line with those we estimate for the current National Priorities List, for which $11 billion to $18 billion in additions to reserves would be required, would the shock to industry surplus not be devastating (although it still would be substantial).

When we speak of insurance customers feeling the impact of sudden and sharp reductions in the industry's surplus, we refer not only purchasers of commercial insurance but to consumers of other types of insurance as well. This is because many of the larger property-casualty insurers also sell other lines of insurance, using common surplus to support all their activities. Thus customers of automobile, homeowners', and other forms of insurance might end up in the short run paying in one way or another for much of any sizable cleanup costs that primary commercial insurers might be required to shoulder.

Any short-run cutbacks in insurance availability and increases in premium rates eventually would be mitigated by the entry of new insurers not burdened with Superfund liabilities. And those insurers who escape having to pay large amounts for such claims relative to their surplus would be in a position to take business away from insurers who could not avoid such costs because those who escape could charge lower premium rates and offer wider coverage.

The critical unanswered question is, how short is the short run? As in many markets, in commercial insurance there are costs of expansion and marketing that inhibit rapid entry and expansion by competitors. Indeed, because purchasers want to be sure of the financial solidity of their insurers, the costs of expanding rapidly in this market may be significant. Accordingly, the length of time during which insurance markets would be disrupted by any substantial addition to reserves for Superfund purposes would depend heavily on the size of the reserve adjustment: the larger the adjustment, the more severe the impact on the capital positions of many insurers, and thus the longer any disruptive effects would be felt.

The Role of Reinsurance

In outlining the effects of Superfund liability on primary insurers, we may have been unduly pessimistic to the extent that the insurers are able to gain reimbursement from reinsurers for at least some of their costs. However, the mitigating effect of reinsurance may be diluted. First, if primary insurers eventually are held liable for some portion of cleanup costs, they may not be able to collect from reinsurers for some time. For this reason state regulators may be reluctant to give primary insurers credit for reinsurance by reducing the amount of reserves that insurers otherwise would be required to set aside.

Second, even if some reinsurers eventually are required to reimburse primary insurers for cleanup claims, reimbursements would only kick in for claims above the substantial thresholds or deductibles typically written into reinsurance contracts. And third, the reinsurance industry itself has far less capital, and thus less ability to pay claims, than the primary insurance industry. At year-end 1991 the U.S. reinsurance industry had less than $14 billion in total surplus, less than one-sixth of the capital held by the forty-eight largest primary insurance groups providing commercial liability insurance.[23]

Although there is no public information to confirm it, our conversations with industry experts indicate that foreign reinsurers also may be exposed to substantial liability for Superfund remediation costs. However, foreign reinsurers also have limited resources. The best-known, the Lloyd's syndicates, had $13 billion in total capital in 1993; but they also have had a series of well-publicized losses and related financial troubles.[24]

Thus even if it is available and required to be supplied, reinsurance would leave primary insurers with a substantial portion of any cleanup liability they are initially forced to bear. And, even if reinsurers were compelled to add "only" several billion dollars to their reserves (or what could be a small share of the primary insurance industry's burden for Superfund remediation), the adverse effects on the reinsurers could be disproportionately large. Although the reinsurers' contribution would ease the pain suffered by the primary insurers, any significant reduction in the reinsurance industry's capacity to underwrite the large risks primary carriers do not choose to bear would reverberate in the primary market itself because reinsurers could be expected to withdraw coverage. In that event, primary insurers would be compelled to reduce their coverage too. In the end, consumers would pay, either with much higher premiums or through reduced coverage.

In sum, regardless of whether the insurance industry is ultimately held responsible for reimbursing responsible parties for the costs of cleaning up Superfund sites, insurers are likely to continue bearing substantial transaction costs. Indeed, it is possible that these costs could be larger than any claims for cleanup expenses that insurers might be required to honor. Although consumers of commercial insurance might not pay directly for any added expenses insurers incur for their hazardous waste costs, consumers might pay indirectly in the short run to the extent that insurers are required to establish reserves of sufficient size to force cutbacks in coverage and thus higher premiums.

Mitigating Impacts through Regulatory Policy

One seemingly straightforward way to avoid potentially disruptive short-run effects on insurance markets would be for regulators to refrain from requiring insurers to establish large reserves for site remediation costs, even if such action might be actuarially appropriate. In effect, this is the regulatory policy now in place. Although it is generally acknowledged that insurers will bear some portion of Superfund cleanup costs, there has been no concerted attempt to force them to set aside appropriate reserves. The drawback to this approach is that a large percentage of insurers' outlays go to transaction costs rather than to cleanup.

Continuing the same policy will not prevent insurers held liable for cleanup costs from suffering a long-run erosion in capital relative to what they otherwise would have had, but the consequences from any such deterioration would be felt gradually, and mostly without public notice. In contrast, any sudden decision by state insurance regulators, federal securities regulators, or accountants to compel insurers to establish larger reserves for future cleanup costs and related legal expenses could have immediate and more disruptive consequences.

If insurers were to establish significantly larger reserves for Superfund-related costs, thus triggering higher short-run costs or restricted coverage for consumers, Congress might be motivated to make dramatic changes in the liability-based system for financing the Superfund. Whether Congress would do so in the absence of a crisis, we choose not to predict.

Mitigating Impacts through Changes in Superfund Liability

Another way to mitigate the potentially disruptive effects of Superfund-related costs on the property-casualty insurance industry would be to replace all or a substantial portion of the current liability-based method of financing Superfund cleanups with some type of tax or fee. As discussed earlier in this chapter, under the Clinton administration's proposal (H.R. 3800) Superfund's liability standards per se would not be changed, but insurers would be taxed to finance the environmental insurance resolution fund. The EIRF would then be used to reimburse responsible parties for a portion of their Superfund costs, thus resolving their insurance claims.

For simplicity, in chapter 4 we estimated the effects of such a tax under the assumption that it would be assessed on all current property-casualty insurance premiums. The administration's proposed Superfund plan differs from the one evaluated in chapter 4 in that it would place a lower tax (0.20 percent) on premiums charged during 1971–85 (when it was not as clear that responsible parties were subject to joint and several liability) than on premiums charged in future years (when liability is clearer) when the tax would rise to 0.34 percent. The administration proposal places no tax on premiums charged from 1986 to 1994.[25]

The net impact of any tax or assessment based on premiums obviously depends on its size. The estimates in chapter 4, which assume a single tax on all current insurance premiums, suggest that for each $1 billion in annual revenue, property-casualty premium rates (gross of tax) would rise by approximately 1 percent if workers' compensation insurance were included in the taxable base, and by approximately 2 percent if workers' compensation were excluded. In either case, to the extent any tax or assessment is passed on, insurance consumers rather than shareholders would ultimately bear the burden of the tax.

The introduction of a tax on premiums could affect the volume of insurance provided by traditional suppliers of property-casualty insurance, whose premiums would be subject to the tax. In recent years, commercial firms have increasingly defected from the traditional market to the so-called alternative market by insuring themselves (self-insurance) or by forming cooperatives with similarly situated firms in the same industry. Any tax on premiums assessed only on traditional insurance could be expected to accelerate this trend, although by how much is difficult to say because we know of no reliable estimates of the price elasticity of demand for traditional commercial insurance. A key point, however, is that those customers the traditional insurers could lose would most likely be the best risks, leaving the riskiest customers behind and thus exposing the insurers themselves to greater risks in the future.

In principle, any loss in business could be avoided if the insurance provided by the alternative suppliers were subject to an equivalent level of taxation. In practice it would be difficult to design such a tax system, especially for firms that self-insure and accordingly make no payments of insurance premiums to another insurer.

Traditional insurers clearly would benefit from any changes to the Comprehensive Environmental Response, Compensation, and Liability Act that would reduce the liability exposure of responsible parties because insurers are exposed to cleanup expenses and transaction costs only to the extent that insured responsible parties are made directly liable for cleanup. How much insurers would benefit would depend on the nature of the liability change.

One of the major goals of the environmental insurance resolution fund from a public policy standpoint is to reduce transaction costs. As discussed in chapter 3, the EIRF would likely lead to reduced transaction costs for responsible parties, but it is unclear whether there would be similar reductions for insurers. Insurers' transaction costs fall primarily into two categories: reimbursement of responsible parties' defense costs and the insurers' own legal costs for coverage disputes. According to research by RAND, reimbursement of responsible parties' defense costs can be expected to constitute 42 percent of insurers' transaction costs once site cleanups are complete. The costs of coverage disputes will constitute 48 percent of insurers' transaction costs. The remaining 10 percent of the costs is for insurers' internal claims investigations. It seems certain that the defense costs of responsible parties would decrease under H.R. 3800 as the allocation of costs among responsible parties and with the government became streamlined. Thus insurers should see a real decrease in their own transaction costs. However, it is not clear that there would be fewer coverage disputes between responsible parties and insurers, and thus less litigation between them. The environmental insurance resolution fund would cover cleanup costs only for sites on the National Priorities List; cleanup costs for non-NPL sites (those cleaned up under state Superfund programs or voluntarily by responsible parties) would not be covered. Insurance coverage litigation relates to the contract between the insurer and the insured, that is, the responsible party. Thus these disputes are not site specific. As a result, it is possible that H.R. 3800 would have little effect on the magnitude of insurers' costs for coverage disputes.

Similar concerns plague the legislation supported by the Alliance for a Superfund Action Partnership. That proposal, which would have an augmented trust fund pay for the cost of cleaning up all hazardous substances deposited before a certain date at multiparty sites, addresses

Table 5-2. *Estimated Insurers' Annual Transaction Costs under Five Options*
Millions of dollars unless otherwise specified

	Type of transaction cost			
Option	*Responsible party reimbursement*	*Coverage disputes*	*Claims investigation*	*Total*
Option 1 (status quo)				
Transaction cost	260.0	298.0	62.0	620.0
Option 2 (co-disposal)				
Transaction cost	195.0	283.1	46.5	524.6
Percent of status quo	75	95	75	85
Option 3 ASAP 1 (pre-1980)				
Transaction cost	130.0	268.2	31.0	429.2
Percent of status quo	50	90	50	69
Option 4 ASAP 2 (pre-1987)				
Transaction cost	65.0	253.3	15.5	333.8
Percent of status quo	25	85	25	54
Option 5 H.R. 3800				
Transaction cost	65.0	238.4	15.5	318.9
Percent of status quo	25	80	25	51

Source: Authors' calculations

cleanup costs only at National Priorities List sites. Thus to the extent that responsible parties find it in their financial interest to sue their insurers for coverage for single-party sites and for non-NPL sites, coverage disputes will continue.

In table 5-2 we make crude estimates of the likely effects on insurers' transaction costs of each of the liability alternatives we have examined, focusing only on the cost of cleaning up nonfederal sites now on the NPL. Estimates of insurer transaction costs for the status quo (option 1) are based on the assumption that $800 million of the estimated $7 billion in costs (table 5-1 for the mid-range option for current NPL sites) have been incurred, leaving $6.2 billion in insurer transaction costs yet to be incurred. As with our estimates of responsible parties' liability costs, we assume these costs to be spread over ten years, bringing annual insurer transaction costs to $620 million. We derive our estimates of the annual cost of each of the three categories of transaction costs by multiplying our estimate of total annual transaction costs by the RAND estimates of how these costs are distributed. This results in the following estimates:

Type of transaction cost	Insurers' transaction costs	
	Percent	*Millions of dollars*
Responsible party reimbursement	42	260.0
Coverage disputes	48	298.0
Claims investigation	10	62.0
Total	100	620.0

To estimate the likely effect of each of the liability alternatives on insurers' transaction costs, we make crude estimates about how the magnitude of each liability alternative is likely to affect each of the three types of insurer transaction costs: reimbursement of responsible parties, disputes over coverage, and claims investigations. For example, we assume that responsible party reimbursement will decrease 25 percent (leaving 75 percent of costs) under option 2 (co-disposal) because approximately 25 percent of sites would be released from liability under this approach. This would markedly decrease responsible parties' legal costs, and thus the costs reimbursed by insurers. Under options 3, 4, and 5, we assume greater reductions in responsible parties' transaction costs and thus in insurers' reimbursement expenditures. We expect much less dramatic decreases in insurers' costs for coverage disputes. As noted earlier, all the liability alternatives that retain liability for large numbers of sites (such as single-party sites and non-NPL sites) can be expected to do little to reduce coverage disputes. Finally, we apply the same percentages as we did for responsible parties' reimbursement to estimate decreases in insurer costs for claims investigations. As table 5-2 also shows, option 2 would result in a marked but not dramatic reduction in insurers' transaction costs—about 15 percent. The reductions are much deeper for options 3, 4, and 5—31 percent, 46 percent, and 49 percent, respectively, according to our estimates.

CHAPTER SIX

Conclusions

To this point we have presented a great deal of information about the Superfund program and its economic effects, both in the aggregate and at the level of several important industries. Now we pull together our analyses and the conclusions we have reached.

The best way to begin is by summarizing in tabular form some of the findings from earlier chapters. Table 6-1 presents our estimates of the total direct annual expenditures associated with those nonfederal sites currently on the National Priorities List under each of the liability regimes considered in this book. The total expenditures are broken down into five categories: those for cleanup liability (the costs incurred directly by responsible parties for site study and remediation); Superfund tax payments (for the petroleum, chemical, and corporate environmental taxes, and for the proposed environmental insurance resolution fund in H.R. 3800); general revenues (which we assume to be $250 million each year under each of the alternatives); transaction costs for responsible parties; and transaction costs for insurers.

Several important conclusions emerge from table 6-1. Perhaps the most notable is the absence of any significant difference among the total annual costs associated with the financing options we have explored. The cost difference between the most expensive option—the status quo (current Superfund program)—and the least expensive—the Alliance for a Superfund Action Partnership (ASAP 2) proposal that would eliminate liability for all wastes disposed of before 1987 at all multiparty sites on the NPL—is less than 4 percent. Even by Washington standards

Table 6-1. *Estimated Annual Direct Superfund Expenditures for Current NPL Sites under Five Options*
Millions of dollars unless otherwise specified

Type of expenditure	Option 1 status quo	Option 2 co-disposal	Option 3 ASAP-1 (pre-1980)	Option 4 ASAP-2 (pre-1987)	Option 5 H.R. 3800
Cleanup liability	1,559.1	1,173.1	711.8	443.0	911.1
Taxes	1,329.0	1,811.4	2,388.0	2,724.0	2,047.0ᵃ
General revenues	250.0	250.0	250.0	250.0	250.0
Responsible party transaction costs	418.5	297.7	165.9	90.6	333.8
Insurer transaction costsᵇ	360.0	329.0	299.0	268.0	254.0
Total	3,916.6	3,861.2	3,814.7	3,775.6	3,795.9
Private sector transaction costs as percent of total costs	20	16	12	9	15

Source: For cleanup liability and responsible party transaction costs, RFF NPL Database, 1994; for taxes, general revenues, and insurer transaction costs, authors' calculations.

a. EIRF taxes included in taxes for H.R. 3800.

b. Insurer transaction costs do not include reimbursement of responsible party defense costs, as these costs are captured under responsible party transaction costs.

this is a remarkably small difference to be giving rise to vigorous debate over the appropriate direction for future policy under Superfund.

Another interesting point is that, according to our estimates, total annual spending for the cleanup of the 1,134 National Priorities List sites considered in this book comes to about $4 billion under each of the options; this figure includes our estimate of annual transaction costs incurred by responsible parties and insurers. If one throws in another $2 billion a year for Superfund-related cleanups by the Department of Energy and the Department of Defense, total annual spending pursuant to Superfund would be about $6 billion. (Total cleanup spending by DOE and DOD exceeds $2 billion annually, but the amount includes cleanup activities under the federal Resource Conservation and Recovery Act and various state cleanup statutes.)

We call attention to this total for the following reason. Total annual spending in the United States to comply with all federal environmental regulation was estimated to be nearly $135 billion in 1992, according to the Environmental Protection Agency.[1] This includes spending necessitated by the Clean Air and Clean Water Acts, the Safe Drinking Water Act, the Resource Conservation and Recovery Act, the Toxic

Substances Control Act, the Federal Insecticide, Fungicide, and Rodenticide Act, and Superfund. This means that Superfund-related compliance expenditures account for less than one out of every twenty dollars spent for environmental protection in the United States each year. Yet anyone following the Superfund debate during 1993–94, either in Congress or in the press, would have received a very different impression of Superfund's contribution to overall environmental spending. From these debates one would have inferred that Superfund was by far the most burdensome of all federal environmental statutes, though the facts support almost the opposite conclusion.

Why such controversy over the size of the Superfund program, and especially over the competing plans to reform it? It is not irrational for responsible parties and insurers to object even to relatively small cleanup expenditures as long as they believe that those moneys are being misspent. Clearly, many of those caught up in the Superfund liability net share this sentiment and believe that the health and environmental risks at many Superfund sites are trivial. But environmentalists, some government officials, and others point to the emergency removals and completed remedial actions under Superfund and to the voluntary cleanups they believe Superfund has spawned as indicators of the success of the program. In essence, determining the appropriate size of the program involves comparing the benefits and costs associated with it. But this assessment is well beyond the scope of this book.

Turning to the bickering over the proposed changes to Superfund's liability provisions, the reason for controversy is clearer still. Although the total annual costs of the five alternatives considered here differ very little, just who pays and how they pay do vary in important ways. In other words, although total spending stays about the same under any of the alternatives, the companies and industries doing the spending can vary substantially.

For instance, under the liability provisions of option 1 (the status quo), we estimate that responsible parties will spend about $1.6 billion a year for the next ten years on remedial actions at Superfund sites. Should Superfund's liability provisions be changed to resemble those under option 4 (ASAP 2), annual cleanup spending by responsible parties would fall to an estimated $443 million, as shown in table 6-1 —a reduction of about $1.2 billion annually, or 72 percent. The percentage difference between those same two options in terms of the transaction costs to be incurred by responsible parties is larger still, with option 4 representing a 78 percent reduction. The Clinton administration's changes proposed in H.R. 3800 (option 5) would reduce the sum of cleanup liabilities and transaction costs to responsible parties by more than $700 million annually when compared to the present liability standards. This helps explain why responsible parties find it worth spending time and money to influence the congressional debate.

To some extent, what Congress giveth, it also taketh away. Thus even though cleanup and transaction costs for responsible parties would be substantially lower under the liability provisions of options 4 or 5 than under the status quo, Superfund taxes must increase to cover the costs of the cleanups shifted to the trust fund under these or other alternatives that would limit liability when compared to the present arrangement. We estimate that Superfund taxes would increase from about $1.3 billion annually under the status quo to about $2.7 billion a year under option 4, slightly more than a doubling. Under option 5, the taxes would increase to about $2 billion annually (which would include funding for an environmental insurance resolution fund, or EIRF), an increase of more than 50 percent.

The firms forced to pay higher taxes under any of the alternatives to the status quo would not necessarily be the same ones that would be relieved of Superfund liability; understanding this is key to understanding controversy regarding the Superfund program. Consider a profitable corporation with little or no Superfund liability. Even if this firm was in some business other than petroleum refining or chemical manufacturing, it would still be paying the corporate environmental tax. The larger its profits, the greater its tax payments. A firm thus situated would gain virtually nothing from a relaxation of Superfund's liability standards, but would pay more in taxes if the corporate environmental tax was increased to pay for cleanup of additional sites using trust fund money. (This effect would be more pronounced if the firm also happened to be paying the petroleum or chemical feedstocks tax.)

By the same token, a firm with considerable Superfund liability under the current law might be willing to pay more in corporate environmental taxes each year in exchange for having its sites cleaned up through the use of Superfund trust fund revenues (rather than through its contributions and those of other responsible parties). In other words, even a shell game in which sites were moved out of the liability system and into an enlarged trust fund would have substantially different effects on individual firms. Accordingly, companies have taken strongly contrasting positions on Superfund reform depending on their special circumstances.

For several reasons, even this picture is a bit misleading. First, consider the distinction drawn in this book between the eventual incidence of cleanup and transaction costs on the one hand and Superfund taxes on the other. As one moves from option 1 to options 2, 3, 4, or 5, cleanup liability falls and Superfund taxes rise. Not only would this change affect firms in quite different ways, depending on their special circumstances, but it would also mean a general shift in ultimate incidence away from the shareholders of the affected firms and to the consumers of the intermediate and final products these firms produce. To repeat a point, this is because Superfund taxes affect all firms doing business, but Superfund liabilities vary significantly even among firms in the same industry. Thus taxes are likely to be passed forward but liabilities must be absorbed by shareholders. (The one exception to this rule would be any retroactive tax that Congress might enact, such as the proposed tax on commercial liability insurance written between 1971 and 1985 that is part of H.R. 3800. Because this tax would not be paid by any new insurer, it could not be passed forward in higher insurance prices; rather, it would fall on shareholders of the taxed insurance companies.)

In another respect table 6-1 presents an incomplete picture. The table shows transaction costs that result from the liability component of Superfund's financing scheme but not the administrative and compliance costs incurred as a result of tax financing. Each additional tax instrument imposes a fixed annual cost on those paying the tax—the cost of filling out forms and calculating tax liabilities. We have shown that the compliance costs for the corporate environmental tax might well exceed the revenue from the tax. The personal income tax uses one tax instrument to collect approximately $500 billion a year, yet Superfund uses three tax instruments to collect $1.3 billion annually.[2] So although Congress could save some transaction costs by switching from a liability-based financing scheme to a tax-based one, the savings in transaction costs might easily be lost by the additional costs of collecting new taxes, which we do not estimate here. Moreover, additional savings could be obtained by switching from many (and complicated) Superfund taxes to few (and simple) taxes to raise the revenues needed for the government's portion of the Superfund program. To repeat another point, because the three existing Superfund taxes generate relatively small amounts of money, it might have made sense at the outset of the Superfund program in 1980 to fund the trust fund entirely with general revenues.

Questions about the cost-effectiveness of multiple taxes to raise a relatively small amount of revenue are relevant to the current debate over an environmental insurance resolution fund, proposed by the Clinton administration in H.R. 3800, and an EIRF role in a revised Superfund financing system. One of the major controversies during the 1993–94 Superfund reauthorization debate concerned what part of cleanup costs should be paid for by responsible parties and what part by their insurers. Because the EIRF would reduce the responsible parties' defense costs, as well as the likelihood of litigation between insurers and responsible parties holding comprehensive general liability policies (see chapter 5), H.R. 3800 would reduce transaction costs for insurers significantly (by more than $100 million annually when compared with option 1, or about 30 percent according to our estimates). For that reason it has some appeal.

Because the EIRF would introduce an altogether new tax, it could be expected to generate substantial collection costs relative to the revenues it would raise. This is particularly true given its unusual nature, embodying both a proposed retrospective tax on commercial liability insurance written from 1971 to 1985 and its nature as a tax on all commercial liability policies to be written in the future. (Thus in some sense the Clinton administration bill imposes two new taxes.) Congress ought to take the likely high costs of collecting these taxes into account during the Superfund reauthorization debate, especially in view of the relatively small amounts of revenue each of the existing taxes currently raises.

It is impossible to tell from table 6-1 what part of cleanup liability would eventually come to rest on responsible parties and what part would be borne by their insurers. As described in chapter 5, that determination rests in the hands of state courts, and different states have decided these matters in different ways. Indeed, one of the major purposes of H.R. 3800 is to bring some predictability and uniformity to this determination.

We make two final observations. First, we have suggested throughout this book that, in principle, it is important to identify the way in which Superfund burdens affect firms in the private sector. In particular, we have made much of the distinction between cleanups financed directly by responsible parties as a result of Superfund liability and cleanups financed out of the Superfund trust fund, revenues for which come largely from taxes on business. In practice, however, this distinction seems somewhat less sharp. Despite our contention that Superfund taxes that fall on all firms in a particular industry (such as the chemical feedstocks and petroleum taxes) can and likely will be passed on in the form of higher prices, those firms actively participating in the Superfund debate seem to be as troubled by these prospective tax burdens as they are by the prospect of cleanup liability. To put it somewhat differently, they seem not to distinguish between Superfund tax payments and cleanup liability expenditures.

Upon reflection, this may not be hard to understand. First, these firms may well take losses during the adjustment period needed for the industry to reach a new equilibrium at the new higher prices (to reflect the new taxes). Second, no one likes raising prices, even if competitors are forced to do so at the same time. Higher prices make the purchasers of products unhappy and bring no extra profits when taxes are merely being passed along.

Perhaps more important, higher prices mean reductions in quantities demanded, especially in the longer run when purchasers can substitute other products for the taxed (and therefore more expensive) products. This means that at least some firms that are economically viable at one price level would find themselves out of business once prices had risen to cover any increased Superfund taxes. Even when the reduction in quantity demanded is expected to be very small (and we emphasize in chapter 4 how small the price effects associated with Superfund taxes are likely to be), it is natural for companies to be concerned about whether they might be the ones without customers in a new, higher-priced regime. Such concerns probably account for firms' being as unwilling to bear higher Superfund taxes as they are to accept new cleanup liabilities.

Our second observation concerns an irony in the debate about Superfund reform. When Superfund was enacted, its liability provisions were justified in large part on the grounds that they embodied the polluter pays principle. Making polluters pay is complicated by the way in which initial tax burdens or cleanup liabilities are shifted—either to purchasers of taxed products or to shareholders of affected firms. Yet some features of Superfund reform may give rise to similar problems. The creation of a tax on insurers to stock an environmental insurance resolution fund is motivated by the goal of making them pay in exchange for resolution of Superfund liability claims. Yet the tax on insurers—at least the portion that would fall prospectively on new commercial liability policies—would likely be passed forward to purchasers, just as the existing Superfund taxes are. Thus an attempt to pin costs on insurers in exchange for absolving them from reimbursing responsible parties would itself give rise to burden shifting and consequent frustration.

In addition, still another Superfund tax would create administrative and compliance costs that might equal or even exceed the revenues raised. These are costs to the economy that contribute nothing to waste remediation. As such, they strike us as similar to the legal and other transaction costs resulting from Superfund liability that have provided much of the impetus for the current reform effort. It is our hope that Congress will be mindful of the full range of economic consequences of changes to both the tax and liability components of Superfund's financing scheme as it proceeds to reform an important environmental statute.

The RFF NPL Database

Staff at Resources for the Future (RFF) compiled the RFF National Priorities List (NPL) Database to allow us to allocate private sector liability and transaction costs of the current Superfund liability system to different sectors of the economy, and to assess how the magnitude and incidence of these costs would change under alternative liability scenarios. The database also enables us to estimate the distribution of cleanup costs between responsible parties and the Superfund trust fund under a series of alternative liability scenarios.[1]

The RFF NPL Database includes information on 1,134 nonfederal facility sites on the National Priorities List. The main source of information for the database, the remedial project manager (RPM) survey described later, includes data on 1,249 NPL sites. Of these sites, 123 are federal facilities, the data for which are not included in the analysis in this book. Data on another 8 sites are included in the RFF NPL Database because they are included in other sources of information used to create the database.

For each of the 1,134 sites in the database, information was assembled on basic site identification, the type of facility on the site, the industry sector most likely to bear the initial cost of cleanup, the number of responsible parties at the site, and the date disposal at the site ceased. We also referred to studies by other organizations (discussed in the section on cost data) to generate estimates of cleanup costs and the transaction costs of responsible parties. We assigned these costs on a site-by-site basis using the site-specific information in the database.

The Environmental Protection Agency site identification number was used to link information from the various data sources together. Information on the type of site was used to assign cleanup costs to specific types of sites and to assess the impact of the alternative liability option that assumes a liability release for all responsible parties at co-disposal facilities (see chapter 3). Information on the industry or industries responsible was used to assign cleanup and transaction costs to specific industry sectors. Information concerning the number of responsible parties at a site was used to estimate responsible party transaction costs, as research to date suggests that multiparty sites have higher transaction costs that single-party sites. Information concerning the date waste disposal ceased was used to analyze the impact of the Clinton administration bill and the two options similar to the one proposed by the Alliance for a Superfund Action Partnership (ASAP), which would release responsible parties from some or all liability at multiparty sites, depending on the date waste disposal occurred (see chapter 3).

Sources of Information

The site-specific information described above is not maintained in a single Environmental Protection Agency database. However, in 1993 EPA, after receiving numerous requests for data about the Superfund program and in preparation for the Superfund reauthorization debate, undertook an extensive effort to collect much of the requested data. In August 1993, staff in EPA's Office of Emergency and Remedial Response interviewed remedial project managers of the 1,249 final and deleted NPL sites to make Superfund data more comprehensible, more comprehensive, and accessible to a broader audience. The information collected in these interviews is available in a single database maintained by EPA, referred to here as the RPM Survey. This database was the primary source of much of our information.

We also made use of five other sources of site-specific information. Data from these sources were compared and integrated to create an interim RFF database, which was our other main source of data. These five sources are:

—Office of Emergency and Remedial Response National Priorities List Characterization Project Database (NPL Characterization Database, November 1991 and December 1992). The NPL Characterization Database contains information on more than fifty site characteristics, including site setting and land uses; industries responsible for generating waste, treatment, storage, or disposal activities at the site; types of waste present; and types of environmental damage reported. All information in this database was collected from documents developed when a site was first proposed for NPL listing. As a result, this information may not be as reliable as data collected later in the cleanup process.

—Office of Solid Waste and Emergency Response (OSWER), Comprehensive Environmental Response, Compensation, and Liability Information System (CERCLIS, December 1992). CERCLIS maintains an automated inventory of almost 38,000 reported sites across the nation and is considered the official repository of Superfund site data. Through CERCLIS, EPA regions report to headquarters on the status of major stages of site cleanup. CERCLIS contains a wide variety of data on both NPL and non-NPL sites. CERCLIS is used for all official reporting on cleanup accomplishments to the government and the public.

—OSWER, *National Priorities List Sites: Alabama through Wyoming, including United States Trust Territories* (state books, September 1991, September 1992). The state books contain brief descriptions of each National Priorities List site. The information includes data on the size of the site, the industries responsible for contamination, threats and contaminants present, cleanup approach, status of response action, and environmental progress.

—Office of Waste Programs Enforcement (OWPE), "CBO/GAO/ RFF Survey" (EPA, 1992). This survey contains site-specific information that Resources for the Future, the General Accounting Office, and the Congressional Budget Office requested on all National Priorities List sites in January 1992. OWPE surveyed EPA staff in each regional office regarding a variety of site-specific information.

—OWPE, Site Enforcement Tracking System Database (SETS, April 1993). The SETS Database tracks names and addresses of responsible parties that receive general notice letters (GNL) or special notice letters (SNL), or both. Not all NPL sites are included in SETS, because GNLs and SNLs have not been sent to responsible parties at all sites. SETS information includes a company contact person, the date notice was issued, and the site where notice was issued. SETS may not include all responsible parties identified at a site because in some cases EPA chooses not to contact all parties believed to be involved at a site.

Information in the RFF interim database was edited to reflect the site characterization that was judged to be the most accurate and consistent. Data in the database were then compared to data in the RPM

Survey. Because the RPM Survey is the most up-to-date and complete source of data on the Superfund program, this source, where appropriate and available, provided the basis for each site characterization.

Site-Specific Information

We describe here the kinds of data used in our analysis, as compiled in the RFF NPL Database. Information on how the National Priorities List sites were categorized is also detailed.

Site Identification

The Remedial Project Manager Survey was used to identify each site by name and to obtain the Environmental Protection Agency's fourteen-digit site identification number. The EPA identification number was used to link site-specific information from the various data sources.

Site Type

Each site was categorized according to the type of facility at the site, using information from the RFF interim database (specifically from the State Books and CERCLIS). Broadly, the sites were divided into six categories on the basis of their most recent use (for example, an abandoned chemical manufacturing plant was characterized as a chemical plant, but an airport built on a former chemical plant site was characterized as a transportation facility). These categories are contaminated areas, industrial facilities, recycling facilities, transportation facilities, waste handling and disposal facilities, and miscellaneous sites.[2]

CONTAMINATED AREAS. Contaminated areas are sites where the source of contamination is unknown or is located off-site and therefore hard to identify. For instance, at several sites water supply wells were contaminated. In many cases the most likely cause of contamination was illegal dumping or leaking underground storage tanks. However, the contamination was not associated with a particular facility, so the site was classified as a contaminated area rather than as a specific facility type. Sites classified as contaminated areas include fields and roadsides where illegal dumping had taken place, residential areas, and wells, groundwater basins, and waterways.

INDUSTRIAL FACILITIES. Industrial facilities are generally manufacturing sites, but also include mining and oil refining sites. Landfilling
and waste handling and disposal activities may have occurred at these
sites as part of manufacturing operations. We identify each industrial
site as belonging to one of seven categories of industrial facilities: chemical manufacturing, including chemical plants, chemical distribution,
storage, disposal, and packing centers, and pesticide and fertilizer manufacturing plants; coal gasification, including coal gasification plants,
utility plants, and coal coking facilities; mining, including mines and
mine tailings, radium contamination, recovery plants, asbestos mills,
precious metal mills, phosphate processors, and smelting facilities; mul-
tiple-industry areas, including industrial parks, complexes, develop-
ments, and other properties and operations; oil refining, including oil
refineries and mud drilling operations; other manufacturing, including
manufacturing plants, printing operations, tanneries, paper mills, asbestos manufacturing, and foundries; and wood preserving, including
wood preserving facilities, wood treatment facilities, and utility pole
treatment facilities.

RECYCLING FACILITIES. Recycling facilities are sites at which recycling is deemed the activity primarily responsible for contamination.
Waste handling and disposal activities may have occurred at these sites
as part of recycling activities. Sites in this category include abandoned
battery recycling facilities, former drum reconditioning facilities, waste
oil recycling facilities, and all other recycling facilities.

TRANSPORTATION FACILITIES. Transportation facilities are those
related to transportation or transportation services, or both. Five categories of transportation facilities are identified: airports, transportation
cleaning facilities, railroads, repair facilities, and trucking operations.

WASTE HANDLING AND DISPOSAL FACILITIES. Waste handling and
disposal facilities are sites where wastes are treated or disposed of or
both and for which landfilling or waste handling and disposal are the
most current uses. This category includes commercial (fee-for-service)
landfills as well as private landfills for use solely by one company.
Recycling facilities are not included in this category. Because the waste
handling and disposal facilities category encompasses such a wide array
of facilities, it has been further broken down into eight subcategories
based on whether the site contains a landfill only, ownership of the site

(public or private), who is permitted to use the site, and the type of waste (municipal, industrial, or hazardous) deposited at the site.

The first distinction is made between landfills and waste handling and disposal sites. Sites categorized as landfills in the RFF NPL Database are those at which there is only a landfill and at which there is no other waste handling or disposal operation. Sites categorized as waste handling and disposal sites may or may not contain landfills, but in all cases include some other waste management facilities such as open dumps, lagoons, pits, or drum storage. Generally, waste handling and disposal sites are described as waste treatment, waste disposal, or waste incineration facilities in the State Book descriptions.

Waste handling and disposal facilities are further divided into municipal, commercial, and captive industrial sites on the basis of ownership and who is permitted to use the site. A municipal facility is a publicly owned or operated facility that accepts wastes on a fee-for-service basis; a commercial facility is a privately owned or operated facility that accepts wastes on a fee-for-service basis; a captive industrial facility is a private site that does not accept waste on a fee-for-service basis.

Landfills that operate on a fee-for-service basis (all landfills except those identified as captive landfill facilities) are subcategorized as co-disposal and non-co-disposal facilities. At co-disposal facilities industrial-type wastes are mixed with municipal or household-type wastes. At non-co-disposal facilities the landfilled wastes are either entirely of the municipal type or the industrial type. Almost all non-co-disposal landfills hold strictly industrial-type wastes; so few commercial sites hold entirely municipal-type wastes that all non-co-disposal sites are categorized together. The distinctions among the different landfill and waste handling and disposal categories are summarized in table A-1.

MISCELLANEOUS SITES.   Miscellaneous sites include all those that do not fit into the other five site facility categories. Miscellaneous sites may have formerly been used as facilities in the other five categories are now used, but have since been converted to other uses. For the purpose of analysis, sites that can be placed in more than one category because they encompass several site types are included in the miscellaneous category. Seven types of miscellaneous sites are identified: agricultural facilities, dry cleaning facilities, military-related facilities, multiple-

Table A-1. *Distinctions among Waste Handling and Disposal Facilities in RFF NPL Database*

RFF facility category	Landfill	Ownership	Fee for service	Type of waste deposited[a]
Municipal landfill	Yes	Public	Yes	Municipal
Municipal landfill; co-disposal site	Yes	Public	Yes	Municipal and industrial
Commercial landfill	Yes	Private	Yes	Municipal or industrial
Commercial landfill; co-disposal site	Yes	Private	Yes	Municipal and industrial
Captive industrial landfill	Yes	Private	No	Industrial
Municipal waste management	Maybe	Public	Yes	Municipal and industrial
Commercial industrial waste management	Maybe	Private	Yes	Industrial
Captive industrial waste management	Maybe	Private	No	Industrial

Source: RFF NPL Database, 1994.
a. Entries refer to category of waste, not to entities or sectors generating it.

operations facilities, schools and universities, warehouses, and all other facilities that do not fit into the other categories.

Industrial Sector Responsible

In identifying the industrial sector most likely to have to pay for the cost of cleanup at a site, we used information in the RPM Survey and the state books. Each site was individually characterized according to the industry or industries primarily responsible for contamination at the site. For sites where the state books and the RPM Survey classifications did not match, we used our best judgment to determine which industry sector was most likely to pay the costs of cleanup. In making this determination we did not take into account third-party contribution actions or the possibility that insurers would repay responsible parties for their expenditures.

For most sites it was relatively easy to assign financial responsibility to one or two specific industries. These sites were generally used by one or two companies throughout the lifetime of each site before operations were terminated; thus it was easy to assume who was responsible at the site. For example, responsibility for a site that was a chemical manufacturing facility from 1974 until it closed in 1983 was attributed solely to the chemicals and allied products category. For the SIC industry categories and numbers used in this analysis, see table A-2.

Table A-2. Industry Categories in the Standard Industrial Classification Manual

Division	Title	SIC identification number	Division	Title	SIC identification number
Mining	Metal mining	10		Electronic and other electrical equipment and components, except computer equipment	36
	Coal mining	12		Transportation equipment	37
	Oil and gas extraction	13		Measuring, analyzing, and controlling instruments; photographic, medical, and optical goods; watches and clocks	38
	Mining and quarrying of nonmetallic minerals, except fuels	14	Transportation comunications, electric, gas, and sanitary services	Railroad transportation	40
Construction	Construction—special trade contractors	17		Motor freight transportation and warehousing	42
Manufacturing	Food and kindred products	20		Transportation by air	45
	Textile mill products	22		Transportation services	47
	Apparel and other finished products made from fabrics and similar materials	23		Electric, gas, and sanitary services	49
	Lumber and wood products, except furniture	24	Wholesale trade	Wholesale trade—nondurable goods	51
	Furniture and fixtures	25	Retail trade	Automotive dealers and gasoline service stations	55
	Paper and allied products	26	Services	Personal services	72
	Chemicals and allied products	28		Automotive repair, services, and parking	75
	Petroleum refining and related industries	29		Health services	80
	Rubber and miscellaneous plastics products	30		Educational services	82
	Leather and leather products	31		Engineering, accounting, research, management, and related services	87
	Stone, clay, glass, and concrete products	32	Public administration	Justice, public order, and safety	92
	Primary metal industries	33		Administration of environmental quality and housing programs	95
	Fabricated metal products, except machinery and transportation equipment	34		National security and international affairs	97
	Industrial and commercial machinery and computer equipment	35			

Source: Office of Management and Budget, Standard Industrial Classification Manual (Springfield, Va.: National Technical Information Service, 1987).

Table A-3. *Aggregate Responsibility for Costs at 230 Not Attributed Sites*
Percent

Industry category	Percent of responsibility	Industry category	Percent of responsibility
Mining	2	Electronic and other electrical	
Lumber and wood products,		equipment and components	2
except furniture	1	All other manufacturing	7
Chemicals and allied products	25	Miscellaneous	8
Petroleum refining and related		Recycling	3
industries	9	Not attributed	39
Primary metals industries	2	Total	102[a]
Fabricated metal products	4		

Source: RFF NPL Database, 1994.
a. Total does not add to 100 percent due to rounding.

If a site was contaminated by one or two identifiable industries only, cleanup costs were either attributed solely to one industry sector or were divided evenly between the two industry categories. For example, if dry cleaners were found to be solely responsible for the contamination at three sites, but at another site a dry cleaner and a car wash were jointly responsible for contamination, the number of sites attributed to the dry cleaner category was three and one-half sites. For those sites where more than two industries were responsible for contamination, or for which we did not have enough information to attribute responsibility to key industry sectors, responsibility was attributed to the industry sectors on an aggregate level.

For 377 sites (most of which were waste handling and disposal and landfill sites) we did not have enough detailed information to assign responsibility to a specific industry (or industries), although in theory others more closely involved with these sites probably could. An example of such a site is a landfill where many parties dispose of wastes. Initially, we categorized these as "not attributed" sites. We did not have sufficient information to attribute any financial responsibility for 147 of the sites. Thus 100 percent of the cleanup costs for these 147 sites was designated "not attributed." For the remaining 230 sites we had some information but not enough to attribute all responsibility on a site-by-site basis. Instead, we attributed responsibility on an aggregate basis (see table A-3). Because we did not have complete information about the industries responsible at these sites, a portion of each site cost remained in the not-attributed category.

It should be noted that the U.S. government's *Standard Industrial Classification* (SIC) *Manual* was last updated in 1987 and does not include several industry sectors that we encountered. The SIC does not include appropriate categories for recycling sites, waste handling and disposal operations, or landfills. Thus, we categorized all recycling facilities according to what was recycled at the site. A site that recycled batteries was categorized as a battery recycler, and a site where drum reconditioning took place was categorized as a drum recycler. Sites where several types of products were recycled were grouped together, as were those recycling sites that did not fit into any of the other recycling categories. For many waste handling and disposal operations and landfills, specific industrial sectors could not be identified because not enough information was available. Typically, these sites were co-disposal landfills where both municipal and industrial wastes were disposed.

Eighty-four sites were classified as "orphan" sites. We did not attribute responsibility for these sites to any industry sector. Instead, 100 percent of the costs were attributed to the Superfund trust fund, under all five liability alternatives (see chapter 3). To identify the orphan sites, we compared those identified as orphans in the RFF interim database with those so identified in the RPM Survey. To address discrepancies between the two sources we used additional information about each site identified as an orphan to determine a final list of 84 orphan sites.

Number of Responsible Parties

Information concerning the number of responsible parties at a site was obtained primarily from the RPM Survey. Sites were characterized according to the number of responsible parties involved at the site: 1 responsible party, 2 to 10 parties, 11 to 50, 51 to 100, 101 or more, and unknown number. If the number of responsible parties was not provided in the RPM Survey, information in the RFF interim database furnished the number. In this analysis these numbers are used in the estimation of transaction cost percentages at each site.

Date Disposal Ceased

The Clinton administration bill (H.R. 3800) and the two alternatives that include the key elements proposed by the Alliance for a Superfund Action Partnership require information on the date waste disposal occurred. Ideally, information would be available on the percentage of waste disposed before 1980, 1986, and 1987 at each site, but such information is not available. However, the RPM Survey provides information on when contamination occurred at each site. For each site, the survey identifies whether contamination occurred during three different time periods: before 1980, in 1980 or later, and in 1987 or later. These data allowed us to estimate whether all waste disposal at a site ceased before two dates—January 1, 1980, and January 1, 1987.

Cost Information

The RFF NPL Database and several studies by other organizations were used to generate estimates of cleanup costs and the transaction costs of responsible parties. These costs were assigned on a site-by-site basis, using the site-specific data described earlier.

Cost of Cleanup

Three components go into our estimates of the cost of cleanup for each site: remedial action costs, site assessment costs, and, operation and maintenance costs. Removal costs are not included. Our estimates of these costs are based primarily on EPA data for the end of fiscal year 1993 and on a report from the University of Tennessee's Waste Management Research and Education Institute, *Estimating Resource Requirements for NPL Sites.*[3]

Most estimates of cleanup costs (including ours) are based at least initially on the cost of implementing a remedial action at a site. At many sites more than one remedial action is conducted because the Environmental Protection Agency typically divides work at the site into multiple projects, referred to as operable units. According to EPA, the average number of remedial actions implemented at nonfederal National Priorities List sites is 1.8.[4] The first estimate of the cost of each remedial action is included in a document called the record of decision. At each subsequent stage in the remedial process—when the remedial design is completed, when the remedial action is initiated, and, when it has been completely implemented—the cost estimates become more precise.

REMEDIAL ACTION COSTS.   We used the average record of decision costs from the University of Tennessee study, shown in column 1 of table A-4, as the basis for estimating the relative cleanup costs of different types of sites. In the University of Tennessee study, 240 records of decision for NPL sites are divided into 16 categories according to site type or activity. That study provides costs by remedial action (rather

Table A-4. *Site Cleanup Cost Estimates, by Site Type*
Dollars unless otherwise specified

University of Tennessee site type	Average record of decision cost	Average site cost (col. 1 × 1.8)	Average site cost as percent of $20 million	Estimated remedial action cost	Additional site costs	Total site cleanup cost	Number of sites in RFF NPL Database	Total estimated cleanup cost
Landfill	11,237,000	20,226,600	99.88	21,932,674	7,108,042	29,040,716	322	9,351,110,690
Surface impoundment	9,127,000	16,428,600	81.12	17,814,321	7,108,042	24,922,363	80	1,993,789,000
Chemical manufacturing	17,433,000	31,379,400	154.95	34,026,191	7,108,042	41,134,233	93	3,825,483,711
Wellfield	3,972,000	7,149,600	35.30	7,752,655	7,108,042	14,860,697	65	965,945,297
Electrical	9,872,000	17,769,600	87.74	19,268,431	7,108,042	26,376,473	21	553,905,938
Wood preserving	17,181,000	30,925,800	152.71	33,534,331	7,108,042	40,642,373	53	2,154,045,778
Waste oil	12,906,000	23,230,800	114.71	25,190,273	7,108,042	32,298,315	19	613,667,982
Leaking container	13,968,000	25,142,400	124.15	27,263,113	7,108,042	34,371,155	15	515,567,319
Manufacturing	3,274,000	5,893,200	29.10	6,390,280	7,108,042	13,498,322	196	2,645,671,107
Asbestos	2,857,000	5,142,600	25.39	5,576,368	7,108,042	12,684,410	3	38,053,231
Plating	3,553,000	6,395,400	31.58	6,934,840	7,108,042	14,042,882	7	98,300,171
Metal working	3,033,000	5,459,400	26.96	5,919,890	7,108,042	13,027,932	10	130,279,318
Drum recycling	6,060,000	10,908,000	53.86	11,828,069	7,108,042	18,936,111	10	189,361,106
Mining	83,683,000	150,629,400	743.78	163,334,697	7,108,042	170,442,739	30	5,113,282,181
Radiological tailings	35,000,000	63,000,000	311.08	68,313,928	7,108,042	75,421,970	9	678,797,727
TNT processing	1,835,000	3,303,000	16.31	3,581,602	7,108,042	10,689,644	0	0

Source: Authors' calculations based on E. W. Colglazier, T. Cox, and K. Davis, *Estimating Resource Requirements for NPL Sites* (University of Tennessee, Waste Management Research and Education Institute, December 1991), p. 45.

than by site) for each site type, based on estimates included in the record of decision. Because our analysis is on the basis of site costs (rather than remedial action costs), we multiplied the costs in column 1, table A-4, by 1.8, the average number of remedial actions at each site, to derive average site costs for each site type (column 2, table A-4). The University of Tennessee researchers found that the average remedial action cost among all 240 records of decision in the sample was approximately $11.3 million. This translates into an average estimated site cost of $20 million.

Since the University of Tennessee study was issued in 1991, the Environmental Protection Agency has collected more complete data on cleanup costs, which indicate that the average cost of all remedial actions to date is $12.2 million a site.[5] This estimate takes into account the growth of costs that occurs after the initial remedial action costs that are included in EPA's record of decision. Increasing the more recent estimate by 1.8, the average number of remedial actions at each site, results in remedial action costs of about $22 million a site. We used this average remedial action cost estimate and the average site costs derived from the University of Tennessee study (column 2, table A-4) to derive cost estimates for each site activity category that are in line with EPA's overall estimate of site cleanup costs.

To determine the relative cleanup costs for different site types, we divided the average site cost for each site type (column 2, table A-4) by the average for all sites (about $20 million), on the basis of work done by the University of Tennessee. The results of these calculations are in column 3, table A-4. Multiplying the percentages in column 3 by EPA's average remedial action cost of $22 million resulted in our estimates of total remedial action costs for each site type (column 4, table A-4). Thus our estimates of average remedial action costs in column 4 are consistent with EPA's recent estimates of average remedial action costs of $22 million, but also take into account work done by the University of Tennessee that allowed us to differentiate estimates of cleanup costs by site type.

SITE ASSESSMENT COSTS. The next step in computing the estimated average cleanup cost for a site was to account for site assessment costs. These costs include the costs of site listing (that is, preliminary assessments and site investigations) and site study costs. According to the Environmental Protection Agency site listing costs are $0.2 million for each site. The Congressional Budget Office has estimated that site study costs (the costs of remedial investigation and feasibility studies and remedial designs) are $2.2 million for each.[6] We increased the site study cost by a factor of 1.8 to account for the average number of remedial actions for each site, which resulted in total site study costs of $4.0 million a site. Thus total average site assessment costs were estimated to be $4.2 million.

OPERATIONS AND MAINTENANCE COSTS. Operations and mainte-nance costs of $2.9 million are also included in our estimate of total site costs. These costs are the net present value of future operations and maintenance costs. Our estimate of $2.9 million a site was based on work done for the Environmental Protection Agency in which the esti-mated present value of operations and maintenance costs for each oper-able unit, in 1990 dollars, was $1.45 million.[7] We multiplied this operable unit estimate by 1.8 to arrive at a site operations and mainte-nance cost of $2.6 million. Then, to present operation and maintenance costs in 1993 dollars, we used an annual 4 percent inflation rate to arrive at operations and maintenance costs of $2.9 million a site.

TOTAL SITE COSTS. Our site assessment costs of $4.2 million and operation and maintenance costs of $2.9 million were added to the estimated remedial action costs in column 4, table A-4. The estimated average cleanup costs for each of the sixteen University of Tennessee site types are shown in column 6, table A-4. Summing average remedial action, site assessment, and operations and maintenance costs results in an average site cleanup cost of $29.1 million. Thus the total estimated site study and cleanup costs for the 1,134 sites in our database is $33.0 billion, or 1,134 multiplied by the average site cost of $29.1 million.

To make use of the site costs in column 6, table A-4, each site in RFF's NPL Database was assigned to one of the sixteen University of Tennessee site type categories, where appropriate. These site types are described in table A-5. We were able to assign 933 of the 1,134 sites (82 percent) in the RFF NPL Database to one of the sixteen University of Tennessee categories. One University of Tennessee site type, TNT processing, is not represented by any sites in the RFF NPL Database.

The remaining 201 sites are those that do not fit into any of the University of Tennessee categories or for which we do not have enough information for categorization. For these sites, a default average site cleanup cost was calculated. The total cleanup cost for the 933 cate-gorized sites was calculated by multiplying RFF's calculated total site

Table A-5. *University of Tennessee Site Types*

Category	Source of contamination
Landfill	Municipal or industrial landfills
Surface impoundment	Improperly stored or abandoned hazardous materials in open areas such as lagoons, pits, or trenches
Chemical manufacturing	Primarily from the manufacture of chemicals
Wellfield	Drinking water contamination resulting from a variety of upgradient sources
Electrical	Handling, recycling, or manufacturing of electrical components such as transformers, batteries, or capacitors
Wood preserving	Wood treating and preservation processes
Waste oil	Handling and recycling of waste oil
Leaking container	Primarily from improperly stored or abandoned containers of hazardous substances
Manufacturing	Manufacture of substances or items not included in the chemical manufacturing category
Asbestos	Asbestos
Plating	Various electroplating operations
Metal working	Metal fabrication or recycling operations
Drum recycling	Drum recycling operations
Mining	Mining operations
Radiological tailings	Improper handling of radioactive substances
TNT processing	TNT processing

Source: E. W. Colglazier, T. Cox, and K. Davis, *Estimating Resource Requirements for NPL Sites* (University of Tennessee, Waste Management Research and Education Institute, 1991), p. 8.

cleanup cost for each site activity category (column 6, table A-4) by the number of sites assigned to that category by RFF (column 7); the results are given in column 8. The sum of these cleanup costs is $28.9 billion. The cleanup cost of the 933 sites ($28.9 billion) was then subtracted from estimated total NPL cleanup costs of $33.0 billion (the total estimated site study and cleanup costs for the 1,134 sites in our database). Thus the remaining cost of cleaning up the 201 uncategorized sites is $4.1 billion, or an average site cleanup cost of $20.4 million.

Transaction Costs of Responsible Parties

The number of responsible parties at each site was used to estimate the responsible party transaction costs for each site in our database. We

Table A-6. *Assumed Transaction Costs of Responsible Parties*

Number of responsible parties	Percent of total cost	Number of responsible parties	Percent of total cost
1	5	More than 50	30
2–10	20	Orphan	0
11–50	25	Unknown	15

Source: Authors' estimates.

assumed that the greater the number of parties at a site, the higher the transaction cost share would be because of increased negotiation and litigation among parties. For orphan sites, we assumed that there were no private sector transaction costs. Responsible party transaction costs refer only to costs incurred by responsible parties; they do not include costs incurred by the government or by insurers.

The estimated percentages of total transaction costs attributable to various numbers of responsible parties are presented in table A-6. Numbers of responsible parties are presented in ranges of numbers loosely based on two RAND Institute for Civil Justice reports.[8] These percentages were multiplied by the estimated total cleanup costs borne by responsible parties at each site to estimate a responsible party transaction cost for each site.

Estimating the Costs of the Liability Alternatives

I N CALCULATING costs of the Superfund liability alternatives, we first used data in the Resources for the Future National Priorities List (RFF NPL) Database to estimate the distribution of total cleanup costs to the Superfund trust fund and to responsible parties under the current (status quo) system (option 1) and then to estimate cost changes that would ensue under the other four alternatives—liability release for all closed co-disposal sites (option 2); liability release for pre-1980 wastes at multiparty sites (option 3); liability release for pre-1987 wastes at multiparty sites (option 4); and the proposed Clinton administration bill, H.R. 3800 (option 5). For each alternative we also estimate the costs borne by key industry sectors and the transaction costs of responsible parties. (Responsible party transaction costs in these estimates include only costs incurred by responsible parties; transaction costs incurred by the government or by insurers are not included.)

The basic methodology and assumptions we used in estimating cleanup, transaction, and overall costs for the 1,134 sites in the RFF NPL Database under each liability alternative are described in the section on the status quo, option 1. Further assumptions made for options 2, 3, 4, and 5 build upon the assumptions made for the status quo and are described in appropriate sections below. A summary of cleanup and transaction costs for each alternative is presented in table B-6 at the end of this appendix. A further breakdown of the projected cleanup and transaction costs attributed to key industry sectors and the trust fund for the period 1994–2003 is presented in table B-7.

Option 1. The Current Superfund Program (Status Quo)

Six basic steps were taken in estimating the cost of each of the five options: estimating the percentage of cleanup costs borne by the trust fund and by responsible parties; taking into account cost savings when responsible parties implement cleanups; taking into account cleanup expenditures by the trust fund and responsible parties to date; estimating the transaction costs of responsible parties; distributing the remaining responsible party cleanup and transaction costs among key industry sectors; and estimating annual cleanup and transaction costs. We discuss each step for each option, beginning with option 1.

Cleanup Costs for the Trust Fund and Responsible Parties

For option 1, we assumed that the government pays 30 percent of the $33.0 billion total cost for cleanup of all National Priorities List sites ($9.9 billion). [1] Because we attributed 100 percent of cleanup costs for the 84 orphan sites to the trust fund ($2.4 billion), the trust fund pays for $7.5 billion of the $30.6 billion in total cleanup costs at the 1,050 nonorphan sites. In order to distribute the trust fund share evenly across different types of sites, we assumed that the trust fund pays for 24.5 percent ($7.5 billion as a percentage of $30.6 billion) of cleanup costs at each of the remaining 1,050 sites. Therefore responsible parties would be responsible for 75.5 percent of cleanup costs, or $23.1 billion, at these 1,050 sites.

Cost Savings Attributable to Responsible Parties

For all cleanup costs attributed to responsible parties, we assumed that responsible parties are able to achieve a 20 percent cost efficiency over cleanups paid for by the trust fund. [2] Thus under the status quo (option 1) we estimated that responsible parties are responsible for 75.5 percent of cleanup costs at 1,050 nonorphan sites, or $23.1 billion. A 20 percent cost savings of $4.6 billion results in a total of $18.5 billion in cleanup costs for responsible parties. Cleanup costs attributed to the trust fund remain unchanged.

Trust Fund and Responsible Party Expenditures to Date

According to the Environmental Protection Agency, approximately $4.0 billion in trust fund revenues had been obligated on site study and cleanup activities at National Priorities List sites as of the end of fiscal year 1993.[3] Data on the amount responsible parties have spent to date on site studies and cleanups—remedial investigation and feasibility studies (RI/FS) and remedial design work and implementation of remedial actions (RD/RA)—are not publicly available. The only indication of the dollars spent by responsible parties on these activities is the value of their commitments as part of settlement agreements. As of the end of fiscal year 1993, the cumulative value of these commitments was $7.0 billion.[4] Because these are commitments for future work, the total value of such settlements is not incurred in one year but over a longer period of time. On the basis of conversations with officials in EPA's Office of Waste Programs Enforcement, we estimated responsible party expenses for site studies and cleanups by distributing the total dollar value of settlements in each fiscal year according to a series of assumptions.

We assumed that responsible parties do not incur site-related expenses until the year after the settlement agreement is signed, that in years 1 and 2 after the settlement is signed, 2.5 percent of the total value of the settlement amount is incurred, and that in the subsequent four years, 25 percent of the remaining 95 percent of the total value of the settlement is incurred each year (that is, 23.75 percent of the total value of the settlement is incurred each year in years 3 through 6). Under these assumptions we estimated that responsible parties had spent $2.4 billion on site studies and cleanup as of the end of fiscal year 1993, out of a total value of RI/FS and RD/RA settlements of $7.0 billion. We then multiplied this amount by 1.5 to take into account an average 50 percent growth in cost that occurs after the initial estimate of remedial action costs. Under option 1, this results in estimated responsible party expenses at the end of fiscal year 1993 of $3.6 billion. Taking into account the 20 percent cost savings achieved when responsible parties implement site cleanups (as compared with costs of government implementation), our estimate of the total amount spent by responsible parties on NPL site studies and cleanups at the end of fiscal year 1993 is $2.9 billion.

To take into account moneys already spent, we subtracted a prorated share of the amount spent to date from each of the 1,134 sites. To determine the amount to subtract, we divided the amount spent to date by the total estimated cleanup costs for the trust fund and responsible parties, respectively. Thus under option 1, trust fund cleanup costs of $9.9 billion are reduced by $4.0 billion to a total of $5.9 billion, and

Table B-1. *Cost Summary for Option 1 (Status Quo)*
Billions of dollars

Cost category	Trust fund	Responsible parties	Total
Total cleanup cost	9.9	23.1	33.0
Cost savings	. . .	(4.6)	(4.6)
Expenditures to date	(4.0)	(2.9)	(6.9)
Remaining cleanup cost	5.9	15.6	21.4
Transaction cost	. . .	4.2	4.2
Total cost	5.9	19.8	25.6

Source: RFF NPL Database. Numbers may not add due to rounding.

responsible parties' costs are $2.9 billion less than the $18.5 billion total given in the cost savings section above, or $15.6 billion.

Responsible Party Transaction Costs

We estimated responsible party transaction costs by multiplying the transaction percentages given in appendix A by the estimated cleanup costs borne by responsible parties at each site. Thus responsible party transaction costs depend on the number of responsible parties and on the costs of cleanup at each site. Under option 1, total responsible party transaction costs are $4.2 billion.

Remaining Cleanup and Transaction Costs

After estimating both cleanup and transaction costs for individual sites, we allocated those costs attributed to responsible parties to key industry sectors on a site-by-site basis (as detailed in appendix A). For those sites where only one industry is responsible, 100 percent of responsible party costs were assigned to that industry. For those sites where two industries are responsible, 50 percent of the responsible party costs were allocated to each of the two industries. For those sites where responsibility is attributed to more than two industries, responsible party costs were first allocated to the "not attributed" category and then reassigned to an industry sector (on the basis of assumptions described in appendix A); see table B-7.

Costs under option 1 are summarized in table B-1. To arrive at annual costs, as presented in chapter 3, we spread remaining cleanup and transaction costs evenly over ten years (1994–2003). Apparent discrepancies between cumulative costs and annual costs are the result of rounding.

Option 2. Liability Release for Co-Disposal Sites

Cleanup Costs for the Trust Fund and Responsible Parties

According to the RFF NPL Database, there are 226 co-disposal sites, of which 6 are orphan sites. The cleanup costs for these orphan sites are already allocated to the trust fund under option 1. Under option 2 we attributed 100 percent of cleanup costs at the remaining 220 nonorphan co-disposal sites, as well as 84 orphan sites, entirely to the trust fund. Thus under option 2, the trust fund pays for cleanup costs of $8.8 billion at 304 sites. In addition, as under the status quo option, we assumed that the trust fund pays for 24.5 percent of cleanup costs at the remaining 830 sites ($5.9 billion). This brings total trust fund cleanup costs to $14.7 billion for option 2. Under this option, responsible parties are responsible for 75.5 percent of cleanup costs at the 830 nonorphan, non-co-disposal sites, or $18.3 billion.

Cost Savings Attributable to Responsible Parties

Under option 2, we again assumed that responsible parties achieve a 20 percent cost savings over EPA. These savings of almost $3.7 billion were subtracted from responsible party site cleanup costs, yielding a total responsible party cleanup cost of almost $14.7 billion.

Trust Fund and Responsible Party Expenditures to Date

Because the Environmental Protection Agency is assumed to have spent $4.0 billion on cleanups to date, we subtracted a prorated share of this amount from each site cleanup cost paid for by the trust fund, bringing remaining cleanup costs to be borne by the trust fund to $10.7 billion. In addition we took into account the $2.9 billion already spent by responsible parties on site cleanups by subtracting a prorated amount from each responsible party site cleanup cost. This results in $11.7 billion in remaining responsible party site cleanup costs.

Responsible Party Transaction Costs

Responsible party cleanup costs at each site were multiplied by the transaction percentages noted in appendix A to estimate transac-

Table B-2. *Cost Summary for Option 2 (Co-disposal)*
Billions of dollars

Cost category	Trust fund	Responsible parties	Total
Total cleanup cost	14.7	18.3	33.0
Cost savings	. . .	(3.7)	(3.7)
Expenditures to date	(4.0)	(2.9)	(6.9)
Remaining cleanup cost	10.7	11.7	22.4
Transaction cost	. . .	3.0	3.0
Total cost	10.7	14.7	25.4

Source: RFF NPL Database. Numbers may not add due to rounding.

tion costs. For option 2, responsible parties transaction costs total $3.0 billion.

Remaining Cleanup and Transaction Costs

After estimating both cleanup and transaction expenditures for individual sites, we allocated those costs to key industry sectors on a site-by-site basis (as described for option 1); see table B-7.

Costs under option 2 are summarized in table B-2. To arrive at annual costs, as presented in chapter 3, we spread remaining cleanup and transaction costs evenly over ten years (1994–2003). Apparent discrepancies between cumulative costs and annual costs are the result of rounding.

Option 3. Liability Release for Pre-1980 Wastes at Multiparty Sites (ASAP 1)

Cleanup Costs for the Trust Fund and Responsible Parties

As in options 1 and 2, the trust fund is responsible for cleanup costs at 84 orphan sites. For the remaining 1,050 sites, we made three assumptions based on the date disposal ceased at each site. First, we assumed that the trust fund picks up 100 percent of the cost at all multiparty sites where all wastes were disposed of before January 1, 1980, except for the cost of illegally disposed of waste. We assumed that, on average, 7 percent of wastes at multiparty sites are disposed of illegally.[5] Therefore at the 374 nonorphan multiparty sites where disposal ceased before 1980, 93 percent of cleanup costs are allocated to the trust fund. Second, we assumed that the trust fund covers 50 percent of costs at the multiparty straddle sites, where some disposal occurred before 1980 and some occurred later. We assumed that 7 percent of the wastes at these sites are disposed of illegally and that the trust fund is therefore responsible for 46.5 percent of cleanup costs at 453 straddle sites. Finally, we assumed that the trust fund is responsible for 24.5 percent of costs at 223 remaining sites. These sites are multiparty sites at which wastes were not disposed of before 1980, all single-party sites, and sites where the date of waste disposal is unknown. Using these assumptions results in total cleanup costs of $20.4 billion attributed to the trust fund.

Responsible parties were assumed to be responsible for the remaining costs at the 1,050 nonorphan sites. We attributed 7 percent of costs at 374 pre-1980, multiparty sites to responsible parties for costs of illegal disposal, as well as 53.5 percent of costs at 453 multiparty straddle sites. For the remaining 223 sites, we assumed that responsible parties cover 75.5 percent of cleanup costs. Therefore under option 3, responsible parties are responsible for $12.5 billion in cleanup costs at 1,050 nonorphan sites.

Cost Savings Attributable to Responsible Parties

Under option 3, we estimated that responsible party cost savings are $2.5 billion, which brings the responsible party cleanup cost total to $10.0 billion.

Trust Fund and Responsible Party Expenditures to Date

After subtracting a prorated percentage of costs from each site to take into account the $4.0 billion spent to date by the government, the remaining trust fund cleanup cost is $16.4 billion. For the responsible parties, $2.9 billion was deducted from total cleanup costs of $10.0 billion, resulting in $7.1 billion in remaining responsible party cleanup costs.

Responsible Party Transaction Costs

Under option 3, responsible party transaction costs are estimated to be $1.7 billion.

Table B-3. *Cost Summary for Option 3 (ASAP 1)*
Billions of dollars

Cost category	Trust fund	Responsible parties	Total
Total cleanup cost	20.4	12.5	33.0
Cost savings	. . .	(2.5)	(2.5)
Expenditures to date	(4.0)	(2.9)	(6.9)
Remaining cleanup cost	16.4	7.1	23.6
Transaction cost	. . .	1.7	1.7
Total cost	16.4	8.8	25.2

Source: RFF NPL Database. Numbers may not add due to rounding.

Remaining Cleanup and Transaction Costs

Responsible party cleanup and transaction costs are allocated to key industry sectors on a site-by-site basis; see table B-7.

Costs under option 3 are summarized in table B-3. To arrive at annual costs, as presented in chapter 3, we spread remaining cleanup and transaction costs evenly over ten years (1994–2003). Apparent discrepancies between cumulative costs and annual costs are the result of rounding.

Option 4. Liability Release for Pre-1987 Wastes at Multiparty Sites (ASAP 2)

Cleanup Costs for the Trust Fund and Responsible Parties

As in the preceding options, the trust fund is responsible for the cleanup costs at 84 orphan sites. For the remaining 1,050 sites, we made two assumptions based on the date disposal ceased at each site. Information in the RFF NPL Database indicates that 624 sites are pre-1987 multiparty sites; that is, disposal activities at those sites ceased before January 1, 1987. Under option 4, we assumed that the trust fund picks up 100 percent of cleanup costs for those multiparty sites where all wastes were disposed of before 1987. But since 7 percent of the wastes at these sites are attributed to illegal disposal, the trust fund is responsible for 93 percent of the cleanup costs at these 624 sites. As in option 3, 46.5 percent of cleanup costs at the multiparty straddle sites (234 sites where some contamination occurred before 1987 and some occurred after) are paid for by the trust fund. The trust fund covers 24.5 percent of cleanup costs at the remaining 192 sites, which are multiparty sites with no pre-1987 disposal, all single-party sites, and sites where the date of disposal is unknown. This brings total trust fund cleanup costs to $23.8 billion.

Responsible parties were assumed to be responsible for the remaining costs at the 1,050 nonorphan sites. At pre-1987 multiparty sites, responsible parties are responsible for 7 percent of costs to cover costs of cleanup of illegally disposed wastes. At pre-1987 straddle sites, responsible parties are responsible for 53.5 percent of cleanup costs. At the remaining sites, responsible parties are responsible for 75.5 percent of cleanup costs. In all, $9.2 billion in cleanup costs are attributed to responsible parties.

Cost Savings Attributable to Responsible Parties

Under option 4, assumed responsible party cost savings of 20 percent results in a savings of slightly more than $1.8 billion in cleanup costs, for a total of $7.3 billion in responsible party cleanup costs.

Trust Fund and Responsible Party Expenditures to Date

Trust fund expenditures of $4.0 billion to date were taken into account after the total cleanup cost to the trust fund was estimated. We subtracted a prorated percentage from each site cost, which results in remaining trust fund cleanup costs of $19.8 billion under option 4. Responsible party cleanup costs of $7.3 billion are reduced by $2.9 billion, the estimated amount spent to date by responsible parties, to $4.4 billion.

Responsible Party Transaction Costs

Responsible party transaction costs under ASAP 2 are estimated to be $906.0 million.

Remaining Cleanup and Transaction Costs

The estimated responsible party cleanup and transaction costs were distributed to key industry sectors on a site-by-site basis, as in the previous options; see table B-7.

Costs under option 4 are summarized in table B-4. To arrive at annual costs, as presented in chapter 3, we spread remaining cleanup and transaction costs evenly over ten years (1994–2003). Apparent

Table B-4. *Cost Summary for Option 4 (ASAP 2)*
Billions of dollars

Cost category	Trust fund	Responsible parties	Total
Total cleanup cost	23.8	9.2	33.0
Cost savings	. . .	(1.8)	(1.8)
Expenditures to date	(4.0)	(2.9)	(6.9)
Remaining cleanup cost	19.8	4.4	24.2
Transaction cost	. . .	0.9	0.9
Total cost	19.8	5.3	25.1

Source: RFF NPL Database. Numbers may not add due to rounding.

discrepancies between cumulative costs and annual costs are the result of rounding.

Option 5. Proposed Clinton Administration Bill (H.R. 3800)

Cleanup Costs for the Trust Fund and Responsible Parties

The proposed Clinton administration bill is the only option that directly addresses the issue of orphan shares at NPL sites. The bill states that the trust fund will pay for the orphan share, defined as the cost share of identified but insolvent parties at multiparty sites. Unfortunately, the bill does not give an estimate of what that share is at an average National Priorities List site. Lacking site-specific information on the size of the orphan share, we assumed that the orphan share is 18 percent at all multiparty sites. This percentage is based on an analysis published by EPA of the financial implications of mixed funding.[6] Because we assumed that 24.5 percent of costs are already allocated to the trust fund for all nonorphan sites (as under the status quo), we applied the 18 percent orphan share to the remaining 75.5 percent of costs only. This results in a 13.6 percent orphan share for all nonorphan sites. Adding the 13.6 percent cost share to the 24.5 percent of costs already allocated to the trust fund under the status quo results in the trust fund's picking up 38.1 percent of costs at the 871 multiparty sites. For the remaining 179 single-party sites, the trust fund pays only 24.5 percent of cleanup costs, as under option 1. For the 84 orphan sites, 100 percent of cleanup costs are attributed to the trust fund. Using these assumptions, we estimated total cleanup costs of $13.4 billion for the trust fund under option 5. Responsible parties cover the remaining costs at 1,050 sites, including 61.9 percent of costs at multiparty, nonorphan sites and 75.5 percent of costs at remaining single-party sites. The total cleanup cost attributed to responsible parties under option 5 is $19.6 billion.

Cost Savings Attributable to Responsible Parties

We subtracted $3.9 billion from the total estimated cleanup cost to responsible parties to take into account 20 percent responsible party cost savings. This results in a total responsible party cleanup cost of $15.7 billion.

Trust Fund and Responsible Party Expenditures to Date

Because EPA has spent $4.0 billion to date on site studies and cleanup costs (excluding the cost of removal actions), a standard percentage of this amount is subtracted from the cleanup costs for each site allocated to the trust fund, resulting in $9.4 billion being attributed to the trust fund for the remaining costs of cleaning up the current National Priorities List. From the total estimated responsible party cleanup costs at each site, we subtracted a standard percentage to take into account the $2.9 billion spent to date, resulting in responsible party cleanup costs of $12.8 billion.

Responsible Party Transaction Costs

After remaining responsible party cleanup costs have been estimated, responsible party transaction costs were estimated by multiplying the responsible party cleanup costs allocated to each site by the transaction percentages presented in appendix A. Under option 5, responsible party transaction costs total $3.3 billion.

Remaining Cleanup and Transaction Costs

Before responsible party cleanup and transaction costs could be distributed among key industry sectors, we took into account another provision in the administration bill: the introduction of an environmental insurance resolution trust fund (EIRF). The administration proposal states that the EIRF would reimburse responsible parties for a percentage of their cleanup costs (20, 40, or 60 percent, depending on the state of jurisdiction) for sites where disposal ceased before January 1,

Table B-5. *Cost Summary for Option 5 (H.R. 3800)*
Billions of dollars

Cost category	Trust fund	Responsible parties and the EIRF	Total
Total cleanup cost	13.4	19.6	33.0
Cost savings	. . .	(3.9)	(3.9)
Expenditures to date	(4.0)	(2.9)	(6.9)
Remaining cleanup cost	9.4	12.8[a]	22.1
Transaction cost	. . .	3.3	3.3
Total cost	9.4	16.1	25.5

Source: RFF NPL Database.
a. Of the remaining responsible party cleanup cost of $12.8 billion, $9.1 billion is attributed to the responsible parties and $3.7 billion is reimbursed by the EIRF.

1986. For our analysis, we used a cut-off date of January 1, 1987 (because we do not have data on a cut-off date of January 1, 1986). We assumed an average EIRF reimbursement of 40 percent because the administration bill calls for ten states each to be in the 20 and 60 percent reimbursement categories, with the remaining states at the 40 percent reimbursement level.[7] We also assumed that 15 percent of responsible parties would not choose to settle with the EIRF and would pay 100 percent of their cost shares at NPL sites. Using these assumptions, we estimated total responsible party cleanup costs of $9.1 billion and a total cost of $3.7 billion to be reimbursed to responsible parties by the insurance fund. The $9.1 billion in responsible party cleanup costs and the $3.3 billion in responsible party transaction costs (calculated before EIRF reimbursement) are then allocated to key industry sectors on a site-by-site basis; see table B-7.

Costs under option 5 are summarized in table B-5. To arrive at annual costs, as presented in chapter 3, we spread remaining cleanup and transaction costs evenly over ten years (1994–2003). Apparent discrepancies between cumulative costs and annual costs are the result of rounding.

Table B-6. *Remaining Cleanup and Transaction Costs under Five Options, 1994–2003*
Billions of dollars

Cost category	Option 1 status quo	Option 2 co-disposal	Option 3 ASAP 1 (pre-1980)	Option 4 ASAP 2 (pre-1987)	Option 5 H.R. 3800
Cleanup expenditures	21.4	22.4	23.6	24.2	22.1
Liability	15.6	11.7	7.1	4.4	9.1
Trust fund	5.9	10.7	16.4	19.8	9.4
EIRF	. . .	. . .	. . .	. . .	3.7
Responsible party transaction expenditures	4.2	3.0	1.7	0.9	3.3
Total costs	25.6	25.4	25.2	25.1	25.5

Source: RFF NPL Database, 1994.

Table B-7. *Projected Cleanup and Transaction Costs, by Key Industry Sector, under Five Options, 1994–2003*[a]
Billions of dollars unless otherwise specified

| | Industry sector | | | | | | | | | | | | Funds | | |
Option	Mining	Lumber and wood products	Chemicals	Petroleum refining	Primary metals	Fabricated metal products	Electronic equipment	All other manufacturing	Miscellaneous	Recycling	Not attributed	Responsible party subtotal	EIRF	Trust fund	Total
Option 1 (status quo)															
Cleanup expenditures	1.7	1.0	3.9	0.8	1.2	0.8	0.6	0.9	0.9	1.6	2.2	15.6	...	5.9	21.4
Transaction expenditures	0.5	0.2	1.0	0.2	0.3	0.2	0.1	0.2	0.2	0.5	0.7	4.2	...	...	4.2
Total cost to sector	2.2	1.2	4.9	1.0	1.5	1.0	0.7	1.2	1.1	2.1	2.9	19.8	...	5.9	25.6
Transaction as percent of sector cost	21	18	20	23	21	19	18	19	20	25	24	21	...	...	16
Percent of total	9	5	19	4	6	4	3	5	4	8	11	77	...	23	100
Option 2 (co-disposal)															
Cleanup expenditures	1.6	0.9	3.0	0.4	1.0	0.6	0.5	0.7	0.6	1.4	0.9	11.7	...	10.7	22.4
Transaction expenditures	0.4	0.2	0.7	0.1	0.3	0.1	0.1	0.2	0.1	0.5	0.3	3.0	...	...	3.0
Total cost to sector	2.0	1.1	3.6	0.6	1.3	0.8	0.6	0.8	0.8	1.9	1.2	14.7	...	10.7	25.4
Transaction as percent of sector cost	21	18	19	21	20	18	17	18	18	26	23	20	...	...	12
Percent of total	8	4	14	2	5	3	2	3	3	7	5	58	...	42	100

Option 3 (ASAP 1)

Cleanup expenditures	0.7	0.4	1.9	0.3	0.6	0.4	0.3	0.5	0.5	0.7	0.9	7.1	. . .	16.4	23.6
Transaction expenditures	0.2	0.1	0.4	0.1	0.1	0.1	0.1	0.1	0.1	0.2	0.3	1.7	. . .	. . .	1.7
Total cost to sector	0.9	0.5	2.3	0.4	0.7	0.5	0.4	0.5	0.6	0.9	1.1	8.8	. . .	16.4	25.2
Transaction as percent of sector cost	18	16	17	21	19	17	15	17	18	25	23	19	. . .	. . .	7
Percent of total	4	2	9	2	3	2	2	2	2	4	4	35	. . .	65	100

Option 4 (ASAP 2)

Cleanup expenditures	0.5	0.3	1.2	0.2	0.4	0.3	0.2	0.3	0.3	0.3	0.5	4.4	. . .	19.8	24.2
Transaction expenditures	0.1	0.1	0.2	0	0.1	0	0	0.1	0.1	0.1	0.1	0.9	. . .	. . .	0.9
Total cost to sector	0.7	0.3	1.4	0.2	0.5	0.3	0.2	0.3	0.3	0.4	0.7	5.3	. . .	19.8	25.1
Transaction as percent of sector cost	17	15	15	19	18	15	13	14	16	24	22	17	. . .	. . .	4
Percent of total	3	1	6	1	2	1	1	1	1	1	3	21	. . .	79	100

Option 5 (H.R. 3800)

Cleanup expenditures	1.0	0.6	2.3	0.4	0.7	0.5	0.3	0.5	0.5	0.9	1.3	9.1	3.7	9.4	22.1
Transaction expenditures	0.4	0.2	0.8	0.2	0.2	0.2	0.1	0.2	0.2	0.4	0.5	3.3	. . .	. . .	3.3
Total cost to sector	1.4	0.8	3.1	0.6	1.0	0.6	0.4	0.7	0.7	1.3	1.8	12.4	3.7	9.4	25.5
Transaction as percent of sector cost[b]	20	18	19	22	20	19	17	19	20	25	24	21	. . .	9.4	13
Percent of total	6	3	12	2	4	2	2	3	3	5	7	49	14	37	100

Source: RFF NPL Database, 1994.

a. Numbers may not add due to rounding.

b. Responsible party transaction cost percentages as a percentage of total responsible party costs are calculated before EIRF reimbursement.

APPENDIX C

The Input-Output Model and Analysis

To ESTIMATE the burden of each Superfund tax on consumers, we must know the impact of each tax on the price of each output. If some industries use taxed commodities as intermediate inputs, then the burden is further shifted to consumers of those outputs. Under constant returns to scale and perfect competition, all increases in costs are passed on to consumers through higher prices. The burden is borne not only by consumers of goods such as chemicals and petroleum, but also by consumers of goods produced using chemicals and petroleum.

To estimate these price effects, we use input-output analysis as developed early in the 1950s by Wassily Leontief.[1] We assume that the national economy can be aggregated into n industries and a sector of final demands that includes household and government purchases. The dollar values of transactions among sectors can be presented in a transactions matrix:

$$(\text{C-1}) \qquad S = \begin{bmatrix} x_{11}p_1 & x_{12}p_1 & \cdots & x_{1n}p_1 & d_1p_1 \\ x_{21}p_2 & x_{22}p_2 & \cdots & x_{2n}p_2 & d_2p_2 \\ \vdots & \vdots & \vdots & \vdots & \vdots \\ x_{n1}p_n & x_{n2}p_n & \cdots & x_{nn}p_n & d_np_n \\ v_1 & v_2 & \cdots & v_n & \end{bmatrix},$$

where p_i represents the price for a unit of product i, d_i is the final demand for output i, and v_i represents the value added of the ith industry. Each row represents the intermediate and final uses of an output and each column represents the intermediate and factor inputs of an industry. For example, x_{21} is the physical quantity of the output from industry 2 that is used by industry 1. With no loss in generality, we use the unit price convention. We define the physical unit of each commodity as the amount that sells for one dollar. Since all prices are one, we can use dollar volume in matrix C-1 to derive the input coefficients. Let x_j be the sum of all demands in row j, a measure of total output. We then define a_{ij} as the input coefficient, the input of the ith good as a fraction of total output of industry j:

(C-2)
$$a_{ij} = \frac{x_{ij}}{x_j},$$

where $\quad x_j = \sum_{i=1}^{n} x_{ji} + d_j.$

As in other static input-output analyses, we assume these input coefficients are constant. This assumption is useful and appropriate for calculating first-order effects on the cost of output from variations in the cost of different inputs, as we do here, but it does not account for second-order effects such as changes in the mix of inputs. It would be necessary to calculate these second-order effects to estimate efficiency effects from tax distortions, or to estimate tax revenue after adjustments in behavior.

As long as profits are included in value added, the sum of all inputs plus value added is equal to the value of gross output. Also, the sum of all intermediate and final uses is equal to the value of gross output. Thus each column sum of matrix C-1 is equal to the corresponding row sum:

(C-3)
$$
\begin{aligned}
x_{11}p_1 + x_{21}p_2 + \cdots + x_{n1}p_n + v_1 &= x_1p_1 \\
x_{12}p_1 + x_{22}p_2 + \cdots + x_{n2}p_n + v_2 &= x_2p_2 \\
\vdots \quad\quad \vdots \quad\quad \cdots \quad\quad \vdots \quad\quad \vdots \quad\quad &\vdots \\
x_{1n}p_1 + x_{2n}p_2 + \cdots + x_{nn}p_n + v_n &= x_np_n
\end{aligned}
$$

Each of these equations is divided by the total output of that industry, x_i, and then rearranged and reexpressed using the input coefficients to find:

$$(C\text{-}4) \quad \begin{array}{lllll} (1 - a_{11})p_1 & - a_{21}p_2 & - \cdots & - a_{n1}p_n & = v_1/x_1 \\ - a_{12}p_1 & + (1 - a_{22})p_2 & - \cdots & - a_{n2}p_n & = v_2/x_2 \\ \vdots & \vdots & \cdots & \vdots & \vdots \\ - a_{1n}p_1 & - a_{2n}p_2 & - \cdots & + (1 - a_{nn}p_n) & = v_n/x_n \end{array}$$

Using matrix algebra, these equations can then be represented by:

$$(C\text{-}5) \qquad (I - A')P = V$$

where
$$A = \begin{bmatrix} a_{11} & a_{12} & \cdots & a_{1n} \\ a_{21} & a_{22} & \cdots & a_{2n} \\ \vdots & \vdots & \cdots & \vdots \\ a_{n1} & a_{n2} & \cdots & a_{nn} \end{bmatrix} \quad P = \begin{bmatrix} p_1 \\ p_2 \\ \vdots \\ p_n \end{bmatrix} \quad V = \begin{bmatrix} v_1/x_1 \\ v_2/x_2 \\ \vdots \\ v_n/x_n \end{bmatrix}$$

and where I is the identity matrix. Assuming $(I - A')$ is nonsingular, the price vector can be derived as:

$$(C\text{-}6) \qquad P = (I - A')^{-1}V.$$

With the Armington assumption, each foreign good is not a perfect substitute for the corresponding domestic good.[2] Because prices are not already set by international trade, equation C-6 can be used to calculate the impact of alternative policies on the price vector.

The intermediate input taxes and the environmental income tax (EIT) are the major financial instruments used to collect money for Superfund. The intermediate input taxes are imposed on each industry's intermediate input of petroleum and chemical feedstocks, as shown in table 4-2. If each intermediate input has its own tax rate (regardless of where it is used), then equation C-3 can be expressed as:

$$(C\text{-}7) \quad \begin{array}{l} x_{11}p_1(1+t_1) + x_{21}p_2(1+t_2) + \cdots + x_{n1}p_n(1+t_n) + v_1 = x_1p_1 \\ x_{12}p_1(1+t_1) + x_{22}p_2(1+t_2) + \cdots + x_{n2}p_n(1+t_n) + v_2 = x_2p_2 \\ \vdots \qquad\qquad \vdots \qquad\qquad \cdots \qquad\quad \vdots \qquad \vdots \quad \vdots \\ x_{1n}p_1(1+t_1) + x_{2n}p_2(1+t_2) + \cdots + x_{nn}p_n(1+t_n) + v_n = x_np_n \end{array}$$

Using steps similar to those used in deriving equations C-3 through C-6, we then have:

(C-8) $$P = (I - A'T_1)^{-1}V,$$

where $T_1 = \begin{bmatrix} 1 + t_1 & 0 & 0 & 0 \\ 0 & 1 + t_2 & 0 & 0 \\ 0 & 0 & \cdots & 0 \\ 0 & 0 & 0 & 1 + t_n \end{bmatrix}.$

Finally, we add the environmental income tax to the model. Assuming that all industries face the same rate of EIT, say t, and that the alternative minimum taxable income (AMTI) of each industry is a fraction, α_i, of the value added of the ith industry, then:

(C-9) $$P = (I - A'T_1)^{-1}T_C V,$$

where $T_C = \begin{bmatrix} 1 + t \times \alpha_1 & 0 & 0 & 0 \\ 0 & 1 + t \times \alpha_2 & 0 & 0 \\ 0 & 0 & \cdots & 0 \\ 0 & 0 & 0 & 1 + t \times \alpha_n \end{bmatrix}.$

One problem in using the 1987 benchmark input-output data is that the transactions are subdivided into a make-matrix ($M_{I \times C}$), which shows how much each industry makes of each commodity, and a use-matrix ($U_{C \times I}$) which shows how much of each commodity is used by each industry (for uses and sources of the 1987 input-output data, see chapter 4, section on effects on prices). To derive the industry-by-industry transactions matrix ($S_{I \times I}$), we must divide each entry of $M_{I \times C}$ by its column sum and then multiply:

(C-10) $$S_{I \times I} = M_{I \times C} \times U_{C \times I}.$$

When we include another row and column for value added and final demand, we have the S matrix of equation C-1. We then derive a_{ij} from the units convention and equation C-2.

Data for T_1 and T_C are shown in table 4-2. Petroleum tax liability for 1990 is divided by intermediate use of crude petroleum by refineries to obtain t_5 of T_1. Similarly, the ratio of tax liability for each chemical divided by total intermediate uses of that chemical provides the t_i for each chemical in T_1. Column 4 in table 4-2 provides the source for T_C in 1990.

Notes

Notes to Chapter One

1. National Research Council, Committee on Environmental Epidemiology, *Environmental Epidemiology: Public Health and Hazardous Wastes*, vol. 2 (Washington: National Academy Press, 1991).

2. Jan Paul Acton and Lloyd S. Dixon, *Superfund and Transaction Costs: The Experiences of Insurers and Very Large Industrial Firms* (Santa Monica, Calif.: RAND Institute for Civil Justice, 1992).

3. Lloyd S. Dixon, Deborah S. Drezner, and James K. Hammitt, *Private-Sector Cleanup Expenditures and Transaction Costs at 18 Superfund Sites* (Santa Monica, Calif.: RAND Institute for Civil Justice, 1993).

4. E. W. Colglazier, T. Cox, and K. Davis, *Estimating Resource Requirements for NPL Sites* (University of Tennessee, Waste Management Research and Education Institute, 1991).

5. Congressional Budget Office, *The Total Costs of Cleaning Up Nonfederal Superfund Sites* (1994).

6. Thomas W. Church, Robert T. Nakamura, and Phillip J. Cooper, *What Works? Alternative Strategies for Superfund Cleanups* (Washington: Clean Sites, 1991).

7. Katherine N. Probst and Paul R. Portney, *Assigning Liability for Superfund Cleanups: An Analysis of Policy Options* (Washington: Resources for the Future, 1992).

Notes to Chapter Two

1. Under CERCLA and the Superfund Amendments and Reorganization Act of 1986 (SARA), state agencies may also take primary responsibility for implementing the requirements of the law.

2. James M. McElfish, Jr., and John Pendergrass, "Reauthorizing Superfund: Lessons from the States," research brief 2, Washington: Environmental Law Institute, December 1993, p. 3.

3. Section 122 of SARA also provides EPA with the authority to develop nonbinding allocations of responsibility, another tool to speed settlements.

4. Nowhere in CERCLA do the words "retroactive," "strict," and "joint and several" appear. The application of this liability scheme has been upheld by the courts under CERCLA.

5. Superfund applies to a broad category of hazardous substances, which may be wastes or products, regulated under the major environmental statutes. Subtitle C of the Resource Conservation and Recovery Act of 1976 as amended regulates the treatment, storage, and disposal of hazardous wastes; RCRA applies to a narrower set of wastes than the substances that trigger Superfund liability.

6. General Accounting Office, *Superfund: More Settlement Authority and EPA Controls Could Increase Cost Recovery*, GAO/RCED-91-144 (1991), p. 16.

7. U.S. Environmental Protection Agency, *4th Quarter FY 1993 Superfund Management Report* (1993), p. III-3.

8. *Comprehensive Environmental Response, Compensation, and Liability Act of 1980*, P.L. 96-510, sec. 104(c)(1)(C).

9. At some sites EPA is implementing a new approach called the Superfund Accelerated Cleanup Model (SACM) to speed up the site study and cleanup.

10. Perry Beider, "Analyzing the Duration of Cleanup at Sites on Superfund's National Priorities List," Congressional Budget Office memorandum, March 1994, p. 2.

11. Department of Energy, Office of Environmental Restoration and Waste Management, *Project Performance Study* (Reston, Va.: November 1993), p. 117; memorandum from T. J. Glauthier, Office of Management and Budget, to Katie McGinty, Office of Environmental Policy, Bo Cutter, National Economic Council, and Robert Sussman, Environmental Protection Agency, Washington, February 2, 1994, attachment B, p. 1.

12. See General Accounting Office, *Superfund Contracts: EPA Needs to Control Contractor Costs*, GAO/RCED-88-182 (1988); Donald F. Kettl, *Sharing Power: Public Governance and Private Markets* (Brookings, 1993), chap. 5.

13. Office of Emergency and Remedial Response, *Progress toward Implementing Superfund, Fiscal Year 1991* (U.S. Environmental Protection Agency, 1994), p. 19; letter to Katherine Probst from David S. Evans, Office of Solid Waste and Emergency Response, U.S. Environmental Protection Agency, Washington, March 31, 1994, p. 8.

14. Unless otherwise noted, all data in this section are for the end of fiscal year 1993; the source is U.S. Environmental Protection Agency, *4th Quarter FY 1993 Superfund Management Report*, pp. I-1, I-2, I-6, V-4.

15. The NPL has become synonymous with the nation's worst Superfund sites, even though NPL listing is required only if trust fund money is to be used for

remedial actions. EPA can use its enforcement powers, and has in some cases, to compel cleanup of sites not on the NPL.

16. This estimate is derived by multiplying EPA's average site cost of $25 million by 1,134 sites. The estimate does not include public or private sector transaction costs.

17. E. W. Colglazier, T. Cox, and K. Davis, *Estimating Resource Requirements for NPL Sites* (University of Tennessee, Waste Management Research and Education Institute, 1991), p. 65. The costs of cleanup are presented in "as-built" dollars, that is, costs are not discounted to reflect the time value of money.

18. Congressional Budget Office, *The Total Costs of Cleaning Up Nonfederal Superfund Sites* (1994), p. 16.

19. Beider, "Analyzing the Duration of Cleanup," p. 2.

20. U.S. Environmental Protection Agency, *4th Quarter FY 1993 Superfund Management Report*, p. I-3.

21. General Accounting Office, *Superfund: Cleanups Nearing Completion Indicate Future Challenges*, GAO/RCED-93-188 (1993), p. 3.

22. The most obvious example is the contamination of groundwater with dense nonaqueous phase liquids (DNAPLs). There is a growing consensus among scientists that what was once thought to be effective remediation—pumping and treating groundwater to remove DNAPLs—does not work.

23. We would like to be able to assess the full societal and economic costs of the Superfund program, but this is not possible. Thus in this book we are concerned only with those costs of the program that can be directly measured.

24. Office of Emergency and Remedial Response, "Progress toward Implementing Superfund, Fiscal Year 1990," U.S. Environmental Protection Agency, 1992.

25. Colglazier, Cox, and Davis, *Estimating Resource Requirements*, table 5-1, shows a total cost of $150.8 billion for 3,000 sites in the base case, an average site cost of $50.3 million.

26. The EPA average is estimated using data provided in the letter to Katherine Probst from David S. Evans, March 31, 1994. Also see Congressional Budget Office, *Total Costs of Cleaning Up*, p. x.

27. See chapter 3 and appendix A for more detailed information on the assumptions we used to estimate site cleanup costs.

28. Congressional Budget Office, *Total Costs of Cleaning Up*.

29. For a more exhaustive definition of transaction costs, see Jan Paul Acton and Lloyd S. Dixon, *Superfund and Transaction Costs: The Experiences of Insurers and Very Large Industrial Firms* (Santa Monica, Calif.: RAND Institute for Civil Justice, 1992).

30. Ibid.; Lloyd S. Dixon, Deborah S. Drezner, and James K. Hammitt, *Private-Sector Cleanup Expenditures and Transaction Costs at 18 Superfund Sites* (Santa Monica, Calif.: RAND Institute for Civil Justice, 1993).

31. Acton and Dixon, *Superfund and Transaction Costs*, chap. 3, also estimate insurance-related transaction costs.

32. Ibid. The 15 percent transaction cost share reported for NPL sites in table 22 of the report is increased by 4 percentage points to account for unattributed costs (see Ibid., p. 45).

33. Ibid., p. 42.

34. Dixon, Drezner, and Hammitt, *Private-Sector Cleanup Expenditures and Transaction Costs*, table 4-1, p. 30 and p. 45.

35. Lloyd S. Dixon, "RAND Research on Superfund Transaction Costs: A Summary of Findings to Date: Congressional Testimony CT-111," Santa Monica, Calif.: RAND Institute for Civil Justice, November 1993, p. 3.

36. See chapter 3 and appendixes A and B for details on how we calculated responsible party transaction costs for the current program.

37. Letter to Katherine Probst from David S. Evans, March 31, 1994.

38. Congressional Budget Office, *The Total Costs of Cleaning Up Nonfederal Superfund Sites* (1994), p. 10.

39. In EPA administrator Carol M. Browner's first appearance before the Senate Environment and Public Works Committee, testifying on the Superfund program, she announced as one of four priority areas an effort to improve data about the Superfund program. Transcript of statement of Carol M. Browner before the Subcommittee on Transportation and Hazardous Materials of the House Committee on Energy and Commerce, 103 Cong. 1 sess, May 13, 1993, p. 15.

40. Speech by Carol M. Browner, administrator, U.S. Environmental Protection Agency, delivered at Cuyahoga Community College, Cleveland, Ohio, November 8, 1993; Office of Solid Waste and Emergency Response, *Superfund: Focusing on the Nation at Large (1991 Update)* (U.S. Environmental Protection Agency, 1991), pp. 8–9.

Notes to Chapter Three

1. Many Superfund reform proposals seek major changes in the way remedies are selected and claim major savings in cleanup costs. For example, an Office of Management and Budget memorandum claims a 16 to 22 percent reduction in the costs of cleanup for nonfederal facilities at NPL sites under changes proposed by the Clinton administration. Unfortunately, there is no publicly available documentation to back up these claims. Memorandum from T. J. Glauthier, Office of Management and Budget, to Katie McGinty, Office of Environmental Policy, Bo Cutter, National Economic Council, and Robert Sussman, Environmental Protection Agency, Washington, February 2, 1994, p. 1.

2. E. L. David, E. B. Nelson, and D. B. McCallum, "Strategies for Reducing Hazardous Waste: What Firms Told Us and What They Did," Madison, Wisc., Department of Natural Resources, p. 9.

3. Public sector agencies such as state and municipal governments and nonprofit organizations such as universities are responsible parties at some Superfund sites.

4. See Environmental Opinion Study, *1991 National Survey* (Washington: 1991); Roper Organization, *The Environment: Public Attitudes and Behavior* (New York: July 1990), p. 1.

5. We discuss only the aspects of both proposals that affect Superfund financing, that is, the liability and funding schemes.

6. Since its introduction, there have been substantive changes in H.R. 3800, especially as related to the insurance fund.

7. Municipal solid waste refers to the category of waste generated, not to the public or private status of the waste generator.

8. Jan Paul Acton and Lloyd S. Dixon, *Superfund and Transaction Costs: The Experiences of Insurers and Very Large Industrial Firms* (Santa Monica, Calif.: RAND Institute for Civil Justice, 1992), pp. 24–25.

9. Other groups have proposed modifications to the administration's EIRF proposal. See statement of Edward Pollack, *Title VIII of H.R. 3800, Environmental Insurance Resolution Fund*, Hearing before the Subcommittee on Transportation and Hazardous Materials of the House Committee on Energy and Commerce, 103 Cong. 1 sess. (Government Printing Office, 1994), pp. 2–4.

10. See Chemical Manufacturers Association, "A 'Fair Share' Liability System for Superfund," Washington, August 17, 1993, pp. 1–2.

11. See Linda E. Christenson, "Superfund Reform Recommendations 1992," Washington, Landfill Solutions Group, n.d., p. 1.

12. See Local Governments for Superfund Reform, "Supplement to Oral Presentation Made to the Superfund Evaluation Committee of the National Advisory Council for Environmental Policy and Technology," Hutchinson, Kans., September 8–10, 1993, p. 4.

13. The features of the current program are described in detail in chapter 2.

14. Throughout this book all government action, including enforcement, is said to stem from EPA, although in many cases the Department of Justice and state agencies are also involved.

15. U.S. Environmental Protection Agency, *4th Quarter FY 1993 Superfund Management Report* (1993), p. IV-2.

16. Municipal landfills may be publicly or privately owned. We exclude from the definition here a landfill owned and operated by a municipality that manages only household wastes of people living in the municipality.

17. Resources for the Future National Priorities List Database, 1994; see also appendix A.

18. Superfund liability attaches to all hazardous substances regulated by the major environmental statutes; a subset of these substances, classified as hazardous wastes, is regulated by the Resource Conservation and Recovery Act. Thus the record-keeping requirements under RCRA may not actually aid in cost allocation at many Superfund sites.

19. *Superfund Reform Act of 1994*, H. Rept. 3800, 103 Cong. 1 sess. (GPO, 1994), p. 77.

20. Office of Solid Waste and Emergency Response, *Mixed Funding Evaluation Report: The Potential Costs of Orphan Shares* (U.S. Environmental Protection Agency, September 1993), p. 5; statement of Jan Paul Acton, p. 14, in *Oversight of the Superfund Program*, Hearing before the House Committee on Energy and Commerce, Subcommittee on Transportation and Hazardous Materials, 103 Cong. 1 sess. (GPO, 1993).

21. Because it is unlikely that all responsible parties would participate in the EIRF, we assume a 40 percent reimbursement for 85 percent of all responsible party costs, rather than for 100 percent.

22. Some of the 230 sites noted earlier are also assigned to the "not attributed" category, as described in appendix A.

23. See appendix A for a discussion of how sites were assigned to the site-type categories. Because categories are not mutually exclusive, we used our best judgment in assigning sites to categories.

24. E. W. Colglazier, T. Cox, and K. Davis, *Estimating Resource Requirements for NPL Sites* (University of Tennessee, Waste Management Research and Education Institute, 1991); Congressional Budget Office, *The Total Costs of Cleaning Up Nonfederal Superfund Sites* (1994). See appendix A.

25. See appendix A for a description of how average site cleanup costs were estimated.

26. Department of Energy, Office of Environmental Restoration and Waste Management, *Project Performance Study* (Reston, Va.: November 1993). This research found that Department of Energy projects cost an average of 32 percent more, take longer to complete, and have larger cost overruns than comparable projects implemented by private industry (pp. iii, v).

27. In its analysis of the cost of the administration bill, the Clinton administration also assumes a 20 percent cost savings for cleanup of nonfederal facility sites implemented by responsible parties. See memorandum from T. J Glauthier, OMB, February 2, 1994, attachment B, p. 1.

28. We define the number of responsible parties as the total number of parties at the site that are potentially liable, not the number that have been held financially liable by the government.

29. Lloyd. S. Dixon, "Fixing Superfund: The Impact of the Proposed Superfund Reform Act of 1994 on Transaction Costs," draft paper DRU-727-ICJ, Santa Monica, Calif.: RAND Institute for Civil Justice, May 1994, p. 35.

30. We included in this estimate the money EPA had spent on remedial investigation and feasibility studies, remedial designs, and remedial actions. Letter to Katherine Probst from David S. Evans, Office of Solid Waste and Emergency Response, Environmental Protection Agency, Washington, March 31, 1994, p. 3.

31. These assumptions are detailed in appendix B.

32. See appendix B for details on how we estimated the costs of each liability alternative.

33. See appendix B for details on the assumptions we made in order to estimate cleanup and transaction costs for the five liability options.

34. General Accounting Office, *Superfund: More Settlement Authority and EPA Controls Could Increase Cost Recovery*, GAO/RCED-91-144 (1991), p. 3.

35. Six co-disposal sites are already included in the eighty-four orphan sites paid for by the trust fund under option 1.

36. As noted in appendix B, this percentage is based on an analysis conducted by EPA.

37. We assume that 85 percent of responsible parties would agree to settle with the EIRF, and that on average the EIRF would reimburse them for 40 percent of cleanup costs. See appendix B.

38. See appendix B for details on how transaction costs were estimated.

39. Bureau of the Census, *Statistical Abstract of the United States: 1993* (1993), p. 552.

40. Data from the input-output model used in the next chapter indicate that the chemical industry is four times as large as the mining industry, as measured by value added.

41. Allen J. Lenz, *The U.S. Chemical Industry: Performance in 1992 and Outlook* (Washington: Chemical Manufacturers Association, January 1993), p. 13.

42. Elizabeth Sowell Haring, "Financial Trends of Leading U.S. Oil Companies 1968–1991," discussion paper 017R, Washington: American Petroleum Institute, November 1992, pp. 19–21.

43. Bureau of the Census, *Statistical Abstract of the United States: 1993*, p. 552.

Notes to Chapter Four

1. No tax was imposed from October 1, 1985, through December 31, 1986.

2. Inorganic chemicals are now taxed at $0.17 a ton plus $4.28 a ton times the portion of molecular weight deemed attributable to hazardous elements. The total tax rate was limited to 2 percent of the wholesale price in 1980. See Price Waterhouse, "Evaluation of Superfund Financing Options," paper prepared for Coalition on Superfund, Washington, May 18, 1992, appendix A.

3. The secretary of the treasury must add to the list substances demonstrated to contain taxed chemicals that constitute 50 percent by weight or by value.

4. Because this tax makes only a small contribution to the total, we do not include it in our input-output analysis later in the chapter. In any case, the input-output model does not distinguish imported items from those produced domestically, and to avoid identifying individual companies, the IRS does not disclose the tax liabilities of the 73 chemical substances.

5. The alternative minimum tax was created in 1986 to ensure that taxpayers with substantial incomes could not avoid paying taxes through excessive use of deductions, tax credits, and other exclusions permitted under the law. Each firm calculates its regular tax at the 35 percent rate on corporate taxable income after all legal deductions, then calculates a tentative minimum tax at the 20 percent

rate on AMTI—a broader definition of income. The firm pays an AMT equal to the excess of the tentative minimum tax over regular tax, if any.

6. Joel Slemrod and Nikki Sorum, "The Compliance Cost of the U.S. Individual Income Tax System," *National Tax Journal*, vol. 37 (December 1984), p. 461. All figures refer to 1982.

7. Cedric Sandford, Michael Godwin, and Peter Hardwick, *Administrative and Compliance Costs of Taxation* (Bath, U.K.: Fiscal Publications, 1989), p. 20.

8. Ibid., p. 142.

9. Plamondon and Associates, *GST Compliance Costs for Small Business in Canada* (Canadian Tax Executive Institute, 1993); Joel Slemrod and Marsha Blumenthal, *The Income Tax Compliance Cost of Big Business* (Washington: Tax Foundation, 1993). Data in Slemrod and Blumenthal "suggest that, in general, compliance costs rise less than proportionately with firm size, so that average costs per unit of size, however measured, are lower for larger firms. . . . The finding of economies of scale in tax compliance costs is common in studies across countries and across types of tax" (p. 6).

10. Andrew B. Lyon, "The Alternative Minimum Tax: Equity, Efficiency, and Incentive Effects," in American Council for Capital Formation, *Economic Effects of the Corporate Alternative Minimum Tax* (Washington, 1991), pp. 51–82.

11. Patty Treubert, Internal Revenue Service, Statistics of Income Division, telephone conversation with Don Fullerton, May 1994.

12. Slemrod and Blumenthal, *Income Tax Compliance Cost*, pp. 5, 7–8.

13. These figures were reported by Patty Treubert, telephone conversation with Don Fullerton, May 1994.

14. Others have suggested that "the cost of computing the EIT could be greater than the current tax liability" for some companies. See Price Waterhouse, "Evaluation of Superfund Financing Options," p. 47.

15. The firms studies by Slemrod and Blumenthal may be even larger, on average, than the 1,952 giants. We have no microdata that would allow us to use their estimated coefficient on size. The $265,330 estimate may be a bit high even for the 1,952 firms, but this bias is probably more than offset by ignoring the compliance costs of the other 10,247 firms on the EIT.

16. Any taxed firm would like to pass the burden on to consumers, but the important question is whether they are able to do so. In the case depicted in figure 4-1, with constant marginal costs and competition, they can pass on the burden. If the new market price were to rise by less than the full amount of the tax, the new price would not cover all of the firm's costs. Until the new price became high enough to cover costs, some firms would be driven out of business.

17. The height of the demand curve reflects the value of these units to the buyer, and the height of the old supply curve reflects the old price paid by the buyer, so the difference is the consumer surplus that is lost when those units are not purchased at the new higher price.

18. With only one small tax and no other distortions, economists always find that excess burden is small. For an illustrative calculation, we ignore the fact that

chemical feedstocks are demanded by other producers rather than by final consumers. Suppose the initial quantity of a particular chemical is 100 million units, the initial price is $10 for each unit, and the demand elasticity is 1 (a 1 percent change in price induces a 1 percent change in quantity). The Superfund tax on chemicals limits a rise in price to no more than 2 percent, so the quantity would fall by 2 percent. The tax revenue would be $0.20 times 98 million units, or $19.6 million. The area of the triangle is one-half the base (2 million units) times the height ($0.20), which equals $0.2 million. Thus excess burden is about 1 percent of revenue.

19. See the report of the Senate Committee on Environment and Public Works on S.1480, July 11, 1980, as described in Price Waterhouse, "Evaluation of Superfund Financing Options," appendix A, note 23.

20. Superfund liability rules might discourage new pollution at potential sites, but the point here is that Superfund taxes appeal more to the equity of who should pay tax than to incentives for pollution reduction.

21. The section on assumptions of the input-output model later in this chapter examines market conditions in the relevant industries. The four-firm concentration ratios (the share of market output of the largest four firms) are generally well below 50 percent, so the relevant industries are adequately competitive.

22. See Roger C. Dower, "Hazardous Wastes," in Paul R. Portney, ed., *Public Policies for Environmental Protection* (Washington: Resources for the Future, 1990), p. 186.

23. See Don Fullerton and Seng-Su Tsang, "Environmental Costs Paid by the Polluter or the Beneficiary? The Case of CERCLA and Superfund," NBER Working Paper 4418 (Cambridge, Mass.: National Bureau of Economic Research, August 1993).

24. For a review of the economics literature on the ultimate distributional incidence of taxes, see Laurence J. Kotlikoff and Lawrence H. Summers, "Tax Incidence," in Alan J. Auerbach and Martin Feldstein, eds., *Handbook of Public Economics*, vol. 2 (Amsterdam: Elsevier, 1987), pp. 1043–88.

25. Several definitions might be useful here. An *intermediate* good is produced by one firm to be used as an input elsewhere for production of a final good. Intermediate inputs are combined with *primary* inputs—labor and capital—to produce a good of greater value. In our input-output model the cost of intermediate inputs and the cost of labor and capital (value added) are used to calculate the *break-even* price—the price that barely covers cost and leaves no excess profits. Under conditions of competition and constant cost, the break-even price is also the *equilibrium* price—the intersection of the demand curve and the supply curve (see figure 4-1).

26. The equilibrium price is also likely to rise with imperfect competition, but perhaps not exactly by the amount of the tax. A monopolist would raise price by less than the tax.

27. "Benchmark Input-Output Accounts for the U.S. Economy, 1987," *Survey of Current Business*, vol. 74 (April 1994), p. 73; Robert E. Yuskavage, "Gross

Product by Industry, 1988–91," *Survey of Current Business*, vol. 73 (November 1993), pp. 33–44.

28. Organic chemicals, for example, are produced using some petroleum products, some inorganic chemicals, and some other goods produced in other industries.

29. For this analysis we use more specific industry categories than those presented in chapter 3.

30. The federal government defines standard industrial classifications to promote comparability of data collected by various agencies. The SIC divide the economy into about eighty industries at the two-digit level (01 through 89), with successively finer distinctions made by the three-digit and four-digit levels.

31. For the most part we do not need the detail of 480 industries, but in some cases we need more detail. For example, the 480-industry matrix provides only 1 industry for crude petroleum and natural gas, so we must separate the tax on crude petroleum, as described later. Similarly, the matrix provides only 1 industry for insurance carriers; in this case the proposal to raise an extra $1 billion in revenue from a tax on commercial property and casualty insurance must be treated as if it were collected from all insurance carriers.

32. Identification numbers in parentheses refer to our categories, as listed in table 4-2, unless otherwise specified.

33. The effective tax rates represent the statutory incidence, that is, the tax that is collected on each of these outputs. We use these tax rates to calculate the economic incidence, that is, the increase in the 41 output prices.

34. Charlotte Dougherty and Elizabeth Gilson, "Economic Impacts of Superfund Taxes," prepared by Industrial Economics, Inc., for the U.S. Environmental Protection Agency, February 1994, pp. 4-2 to 4-6.

35. See, for example, John B. Shoven and John Whalley, "Applied General-Equilibrium Models of Taxation and International Trade: An Introduction and Survey," *Journal of Economic Literature,* vol. 22 (September 1984), pp. 1007–51.

36. These concentration ratios can be found in Bureau of Census, "Concentration Ratios in Manufacturing," *Census of Manufactures* (Department of Commerce, 1980). An analysis of tax incidence without perfect competition can be found in Michael L. Katz and Harvey S. Rosen, "Tax Analysis in an Oligopoly Model," *Public Finance Quarterly,* vol. 13 (January 1985), pp. 3–19.

37. F. M. Scherer, *Industrial Market Structure and Economic Performance* (Chicago: Rand McNally, 1970).

38. This assumption follows Paul S. Armington, "A Theory of Demand for Products Distinguished by Place of Production," *International Monetary Fund Staff Papers*, vol. 16 (March 1969), pp. 159–76. For example, a Ford automobile is not exactly the same as a Volvo or a Mercedes. Consumers can substitute between them, and the extent of demand for each car depends on their relative prices. If Superfund taxes raise the prices of inputs to the American auto industry and thus raise domestic car prices, some consumers may switch to foreign cars. The demand for American cars may fall, but it does not fall to zero. The cars are imperfect

substitutes, which means that some Americans would still buy American cars even at the higher price. Imperfect substitutability is irrelevant for petroleum and chemicals because imports are subject to the same Superfund taxes as domestic petroleum and chemicals.

39. As described in appendix C, our unit convention defines a unit of each good as the amount that costs one dollar. Then the old price with no tax is exactly 1.0, and the new price is itself the ratio of new price to old price.

40. If the original price of organic chemicals (no. 18) was 1.0, then the new price is 1.0008, according to figure 4-2. If this sale is subject to the 0.34 percent tax shown in table 4-2, the amount paid is 1.008 times 1.0034, which equals 1.0042.

41. Because we have no elasticities of demand, this calculation uses the fixed behavior implicit in the coefficients of the input-output model.

42. The new price of organic chemicals rises from 1.000 to 1.004, so the user must pay (1.004) times 1 plus the new tax rate (1.53 percent). Because (1.004) $\times$ (1.01533) equals 1.0194, the cost of this input increases 1.94 percent.

43. An income-type VAT applies to sales minus material inputs; a consumption-type VAT applies to sales minus the costs of materials and new investment.

44. Total U.S. value added in 1990 was $5,522.2 billion, according to Robert P. Parker, "Gross Product by Industry, 1977–90," *Survey of Current Business*, vol. 73 (May 1993), p. 51.

45. *Best's Aggregates and Averages: Property and Casualty, 1992* (Oldwick, N.J.: A. M. Best, 1992).

46. See J. Lon Carlson and Charles W. Bausell Jr., "Financing Superfund: An Evaluation of Alternative Tax Mechanisms," *Natural Resources Journal,* vol. 27 (Winter 1987), pp. 103–22, for an evaluation of several waste-end tax options. A tax on waste disposal is compared to a tax on waste generation in Douglas W. McNiel and Andrew W. Foshee, "Superfund Financing Alternatives," *Policy Studies Review*, vol. 7 (Summer 1988), pp. 751–60.

47. For disposal facilities that met the monitoring and care regulations after closure, the PCLTF would assume liability for damages after five years and would assume all costs for maintenance after thirty years. Tax payments into the fund could thus be interpreted as premiums to acquire later insurance provided by government.

48. See Environmental Information, Ltd., "Interdependence in the Management of Hazardous Waste," Minneapolis, June 1993, pp. 3–4, where it is estimated that 95 percent of firms generating hazardous waste rely to some extent on off-site facilities, but that 95.4 percent of hazardous waste volumes were managed on site in 1989. The implication is that most of this volume is the wastewater of a relatively few large firms, managed on the premises (usually by deep-well injection), whereas relatively many small firms generate small volumes of other hazardous waste that is sent to disposal facilities.

49. Office of Solid Waste, *Report to the Congress of the United States on the Post-Closure Liability Trust Fund Under Section 301(a) (2) (ii) of the Comprehensive Envi-*

ronmental Response, Compensation, and Liability Act of 1980 (Environmental Protection Agency, 1985).

50. General Accounting Office, *Hazardous Waste: Funding of Postclosure Liabilities Remains Uncertain*, GAO/RCED-90-64 (1990).

Notes to Chapter Five

1. Responsible parties have made some claims under other insurance policies, notably those providing commercial multiperil coverage. But, the overwhelming proportion of all Superfund-related claims are made under commercial general liability policies.

2. Some insurers have contested the obligation to reimburse insureds for legal costs related to Superfund cleanups in states where courts have ruled that coverage does not extend to cleanup costs. See Jan Paul Acton and Lloyd S. Dixon, *Superfund and Transaction Costs: The Experiences of Insurers and Very Large Industrial Firms* (Santa Monica, Calif.: RAND Institute for Civil Justice, 1992), pp. 22–23.

3. Quoted from E. Joshua Rosenkranz, "The Pollution Exclusion Clause through the Looking Glass," *Georgetown Law Journal*, vol. 74 (April 1986), p. 1251.

4. According to Kenneth Abraham of the University of Virginia Law School, through mid-1993 thirteen state supreme court decisions had been made on the meaning of the "sudden and accidental" provisions, with six siding with the responsible parties and seven with the insurers. Among lower state court decisions, the tide seems to have been running about 60 percent in favor of the insurers. On the interpretation of "damages," Abraham reports that nine out of ten state supreme court decisions have favored the responsible parties. See also Milo Geyelin, "Knock at Clinton Puzzles Legal Reformers," *Wall Street Journal*, September 8, 1992, p. B 10; Orin Kramer and Richard Briffault, *Cleaning Up Hazardous Waste: Is There a Better Way?* (New York: Insurance Information Institute Press, 1993), pp. 104–05.

5. The initial proposal differed in some key respects. This summary reflects the proposal at the time this book was written. See "Superfund: Parties Reach Agreement over Insurance Fund," *Environmental Reporter*, March 18, 1994, p. 1955.

6. Congressional Budget Office, *The Total Costs of Cleaning Up Nonfederal Superfund Sites* (1994), p. 16.

7. Acton and Dixon, *Superfund and Transaction Costs*, p. 42.

8. Ibid., pp. 32, 42.

9. Lloyd S. Dixon, "Fixing Superfund: The Impact of the Proposed Superfund Reform Act of 1994 on Transaction Costs," conference paper on reforming Superfund, American Enterprise Institute, June 1994, table A.2.

10. John H. Snyder and W. Dolson Smith, "Environmental/Asbestos Liability Exposures: A P/C Industry Black Hole," *Best Week Property/Casualty Supplement*, March 28, 1994, p. 13.

to Cut Agents and Hurricane Exposure," *Wall Street Journal*, June 3, 1993, p. A2; Linda Grant, "Avoiding the Wreckage," *U.S. News & World Report*, June 21, 1993, pp. 49–52.

23. Reinsurance Association of America, *Reinsurance Underwriting Review, 1991: Premiums, Losses and Operating Results* (Washington, 1992), p. 7; and authors' calculations using data from *Best's Aggregates and Averages, 1992.*

24. See Greg Steinmetz, "Alluring Island: New Bermuda Insurers Are Draining Business from London Market," *Wall Street Journal*, August 31, 1993, p. A1.

25. At the time this book went to press, the exact specifications of the taxes to finance the EIRF were under debate in Congress. Thus the description of the EIRF tax here may not reflect its final form.

Notes to Chapter Six

1. Office of Policy, Planning, and Evaluation, *Environmental Investments: The Cost of a Clean Environment* (U.S. Environmental Protection Agency, 1990), pp. 8–21.

2. *Economic Report of the President, January 1993*, p. 437.

Notes to Appendix A

1. The RFF NPL Database includes information on cleanup status and enforcement action that was not used for the analysis in this book.

2. The sites are categorized differently in chapter 3, where transportation facilities and miscellaneous sites are combined in one category, and waste handling and disposal facilities are broken down into four smaller categories: co-disposal landfills, commercial waste handling and disposal, captive waste handling and disposal, and municipal waste (only) landfills.

3. E. W. Colglazier, T. Cox, and K. Davis, "Estimating Resource Requirements for NPL Sites," University of Tennessee, Waste Management Research and Education Institute, 1991; letter to Katherine Probst from David S. Evans, Office of Solid Waste and Emergency Response, Environmental Protection Agency, Washington, March 31, 1994.

4. Letter to Probst from Evans, March 31, 1994, p. 2.

5. Ibid.

6. Ibid.; Congressional Budget Office, *The Total Costs of Cleaning Up Nonfederal Superfund Sites* (1994), p. 29.

7. CH2M Hill, *ROD O&M Cost Analysis* (Reston, Va.: June 30, 1991), attachment F, p. 1.

8. Jan Paul Acton and Lloyd S. Dixon, *Superfund and Transaction Costs: The Experiences of Insurers and Very Large Industrial Firms* (Santa Monica, Calif.: RAND

11. See Amy S. Bouska, "Superfund: A Land Mine in the Insurance Indu *Environmental Finance* (Summer 1991), pp. 177–89. Tillinghast provides ma ment and actuarial consulting services to insurers and the financial service i tries.

12. Congressional Budget Office, *Total Costs of Cleaning Up Nonfederal Sup Sites*, pp. 14–15.

13. Milton Russell, E. William Colglazier, and Mary R. English, *Haza Waste Remediation: The Task Ahead* (University of Tennessee, Waste Manag Research and Education Institute, December 1991), pp. 6–11.

14. Our projections, like those of the CBO, exclude any liability fo damages suffered by third parties, because these do not arise as a result of CEI liability.

15. It is true that insurers are likely to pick up some of the costs alloca orphan shares, because many large responsible parties that have insurance cor may voluntarily assume some portion of the orphan costs to avoid litigatir allocation. But to the extent that the trust fund bears the costs of orphan s the insurers would be relieved of that responsibility. Under the administratic (H.R. 3800) the trust fund would pay for some orphan shares, as noted in cl 3. Many large responsible parties that now self-insure had commercial lia policies before 1986 and thus may be in a position to shift part of their c(the insurers, notwithstanding their current self-insured status.

16. This percentage is well below the RAND estimate that responsible expenditures on transaction costs would total 21 percent of cleanup costs, an below any total transaction cost figure that includes responsible parties and i spending on coverage litigation. Nevertheless, the transaction cost percent our low-cost scenarios reflects the likelihood that many of the issues n litigation will gradually be clarified, so that the transaction cost share shou over time.

17. *Best's Aggregates and Averages: Property and Casualty 1992* (Oldwick, A. M. Best, 1992), p. 185.

18. Ruth Gastel, "Catastrophes: Insurance Issues," *Insurance Issues Updai* 1994), p. 1.

19. Market shares based on *Best's Aggregates and Averages: Property-Ca 1992*, p. 185.

20. A rough rule of thumb among insurance regulators is that at least 3: of surplus should back every dollar of premium revenue.

21. According to 1991 annual report, form 10-K, filed with the U.S. Sec and Exchange Commission (file 1-8323), p. 14, CIGNA had established a of $93 million for environmental pollution claims as of year end 1991. reported in 1992 (*Aetna Reports: Annual Report 1992*) adding $202 mill reserves for environmental liability claims. CIGNA added to its reserves f gation expenses in the third quarter of 1993. In 1993 Travelers establishec ronmental reserves and Aetna strengthened its reserves.

22. Chris Roush, "The Weather Has Home Insurers Running Scared," *E Week*, April 5, 1993, p. 30; Greg Steinmetz, "Florida Challenges Travelers

Institute for Civil Justice, 1992); Lloyd S. Dixon, Deborah S. Drezner, and James K. Hammitt, *Private-Sector Cleanup Expenditures and Transaction Costs at 18 Superfund Sites* (Santa Monica, Calif.: RAND Institute for Civil Justice, 1993).

Notes to Appendix B

1. Letter from David S. Evans, director, program development and budget staff, U.S. Environmental Protection Agency Office of Solid Waste and Emergency Response, Washington, March 31, 1994, p. 5.

2. Memorandum from T. J. Glauthier, Office of Management and Budget, to Katie McGinty, Office on Environmental Policy, Bo Cutter, National Economic Council, and Robert Sussman, Environmental Protection Agency, Washington, February 2, 1994, attachment B, page 1.

3. Letter from David S. Evans, March 31, 1994, p. 3.

4. U.S. Environmental Protection Agency, CERCLA Enforcement Division, CERCLIS Database: ENFR-03: Program-to-Date Settlements, Master Report, Response Settlements Only, RD/RA/LR Settlements Only, All Sites, Activity Summary by Fiscal Year, FY 1980–FY 1993 (March 1, 1994).

5. According to Katherine N. Probst and Paul R. Portney, *Assigning Liability for Superfund Cleanups* (Washington: Resources for the Future, 1992), p. 53, illegal disposal was the primary cause of contamination at 6 percent of multiparty sites. At another 2 percent of such sites contamination was caused by a combination of permitted and illegal operations, so we assigned half of these costs to the trust fund. Thus we assumed that 7 percent of cleanup costs overall are attributable to illegal disposal.

6. Office of Solid Waste and Emergency Response, Office of Waste Programs Enforcement, *Mixed Funding Evaluation Report: The Potential Costs of Orphan Shares* (U.S. Environmental Protection Agency, September 1993), p. 5; statement of Jan Paul Acton, P. 14, in *Oversight of the Superfund Program*, Hearing before the Subcommittee on Transportation and Hazardous Materials of the House Committee on Energy and Commerce, 103 Cong. 1 sess. (Government Printing Office, 1993).

7. *Superfund Reform Act of 1994*, H.R. 3800, 103 Cong. 1 sess. (GPO, 1994), sec. 802.

Notes to Appendix C

1. Wassily Leontief, *Input-Output Economics*, 2d ed. (Oxford University Press, 1986).

2. Paul S. Armington, "A Theory of Demand for Products Distinguished by Place of Production," International Monetary Fund Staff Papers 16 (1969), pp. 159–76.

Index

Tipping fees, 88
Tobacco, 75–76, 80
Toxic Substances Control Act, 111–12
Trust fund: cleanup financing, 13, 14,
    16, 30–31, 40–42; expenditures
    to 1993, 39, 78; funding levels,
    23–24; orphan shares, 14, 28,
    29, 30, 33, 39, 40, 42; reve-
    nues, 55; role, 22–23, 29; Super-
    fund reform options, 40–42, 43,

47, 48; taxation and, 10, 54–58,
113; transaction costs and, 37,
46, 47. *See also* Taxation

United Kingdom, value added tax, 59
University of Tennessee, 2–3, 18, 20,
    36

Value added tax (VAT). *See* Taxation